Aller Retour New York

Henry Miller

ET REMOTISSIMA PROPE

Modern Voices

Modern Voices
Published by Hesperus Press Limited
4 Rickett Street, London sw6 1ru
www.hesperuspress.com

Aller Retour New York first published in 1935
Via Dieppe–Newhaven first published in 1939
First published by Hesperus Press Limited, 2007

Aller Retour New York Copyright © Henry Miller 1935
Via Dieppe–Newhaven Copyright © Henry Miller 1939

Designed and typeset by Fraser Muggeridge studio
Printed in Jordan by the Jordan National Press

ISBN: 1-84391-435-2
ISBN13: 978-1-84391-435-8

Contents

Aller Retour New York

Being the account of a voyage to New York and back
exactly as recorded in a letter to Alfred Perlès,[1]
the distinguished Viennese French writer, who up
till now has held the record for letter writing.

Dear Fred,

I will probably take the Champlain, the boat I arrived on, because it is French and because it leaves a day earlier than necessary. I will bring the stockings for Maggy – and anything else I can think of. Don't know yet about going to the Villa Seurat, but Hotel des Terrasses suits me down to the ground – because it's 13th Arrondissement and no eclogues. Make sure my bike is there. I am going to use it! And where is my phono? I am bringing back some of the famous jazz hits, the crooning, swooning lullabys sung by the guys without testicles. (The popular favorite is: 'I Believe in Miracles.' *Miracles!* How American! Well shit, I'll explain all this in detail when I see you, and have a fine bottle of wine handy, a mellow one, a costly one. Here nothing but California vintages, or dago red, which is vile stuff. One must 'alkalize' every day... I'll explain that too, later.)

So, Joey,[2] what are we going to do for a living, hein? Search me! But I feel that we're going to live just the same. Anyway, I come... The Jew who published my *Glittering Pie* in that revolutionary Dance Program got back at me by entitling it: 'I came, I saw, I *fled*.' The expatriates are anathema to the Americans, particularly to the Communists. I have made myself heartily disliked everywhere, except among the dumb Gentiles who live in the suburbs and guzzle it over the weekends. With these blokes I sing, dance, whistle, make merry the whole night long. I have nothing in common with them aside from the desire to enjoy myself. To know how to enjoy oneself is something unknown here. Usually it consists in making a loud noise. At Manhasset one night Emil and I did the cakewalk so strenuously that Emil dislocated one of his testicles. It was a marvellous night in which we drank ourselves sober. Towards the end I sat down and, striking every wrong note on the piano, I played as only Paderewski[3] himself could play, *if he were drunk*. I broke a few keys and every nail on my fingers. Went to bed with a

3

Mexican hat three feet broad. It lay on my stomach like a huge sunflower. In the morning I found myself in the child's bedroom and beside me a little typewriter made of hard rubber which I couldn't write on, drunk as I was. I also found a rosary and crucifix awarded by the Society of the Miraculous Medal, Germantown, Pa. It was '*indulgenced for a Happy Death and the Way of the Cross.*'

I have had a lot of funny experiences, but few gay ones. When I get back to Paris I shall remember the evenings spent sitting on couches in studios with everybody talking pompously and callously about social-economic conditions – with cruel lapses of Proust and Cocteau. (To talk of Proust or Joyce today in America is to be quite up to the minute! Some one will ask you blandly – 'what is all this crap about *Surréalisme?* What *is* it?' Whereupon I usually explain that *Surréalisme* is when you piss in your friend's beer and he drinks it by mistake.)

Met William Carlos Williams the other night and had a rousing time with him at Hiler's place. Holty arrived with two dopey brothers-in-law, one of whom played the piano. Everybody crocked, including Lisette. Just before all hands passed out someone yelled – 'All art is local' – which precipitated a riot. After that nothing is clear. Hiler sits in his drawers, with legs crossed, and plays 'Believe It Beloved,' another hit of the season. The janitor comes and raises hell – he was an aviator for Mussolini. Then come the Dockstadter Sisters who write for the pulps. After that Monsieur Bruine who has been in America 39 years and looks exactly like a Frenchman. He is in love with a dizzy blonde from the Vanities. Unfortunately she got so drunk that she puked all over him while sitting on his lap. He's cured of her now.

I mention these little details because without them the American scene is not complete. Everywhere it is drunkenness and vomiting, or breaking of windows and smashing heads.

Twice recently I narrowly missed being cracked over the head. People walk the streets at night lit up and looking for trouble. They come on you unexpectedly and invite you to fight – for the fun of it! It must be the climate – *and the machine*. The machines are driving them screwy. Nothing is done by hand anymore. Even the doors open magically: as you approach the door you step on a treadle and the door springs open for you. It's hallucinating. And then there are the patent medicines. Exlax for constipation – everybody has constipation! – and Alka-Seltzer for hangovers. Everybody wakes up with a head-ache. For breakfast it's a Bromo-Seltzer – with orange juice and toasted corn muffins, of course. To start the day right you must *alkalize*. It says so in all the subway trains. High-pressure talks, quick action, money down, mortgaged to the eyes, prosperity around the corner (it's always around the corner!), don't worry, keep smiling, believe it beloved, etc., etc. The songs are marvel-lous, especially as to words. They betray the incurable melan-choly and optimism of the American race. I wish I were a foreigner and getting it from scratch. A good one just now is: 'The Object of my Affection is to change my Complex-ion... ' I'll bring this along too.

At the burlesque Sunday afternoon I heard Gypsy Rose Lee[4] sing 'Give Me a Lay!' She had a Hawaiian lei in her hand and she was telling how it felt to get a good lay, how even mother would be grateful for a lay once in a while. She said she'd take a lay on the piano, or on the floor. An old-fashioned lay, too, if needs be. The funny part of it is the house was almost empty. After the first half-hour every one gets up nonchalantly and moves down front to the good seats. The strippers talk to their customers as they do their stunt. The coup de grâce comes when, after having divested themselves of every stitch of clothing, there is left only a spangled girdle with a fig leaf dangling in front – sometimes a little monkey beard, which is quite ravishing.

As they draw towards the wings they stick their bottoms out and slip the girdle off. Sometimes they darken the stage and give a belly dance in radium paint. It's good to see the belly button glowing like a glowworm, or like a bright half dollar. It's better still to see them holding their boobies, especially when said boobies are full of milk. Then there is the loudspeaker through which some idiotic jake roars: 'Give the little ladies a hand please!' Or else – 'Now, ladies and gentlemen, we are going to present to you that most charming personality fresh from Hollywood – Miss Chlorine Duval of the Casino de Paris.' Said Chlorine Duval is generally streamlined, with the face of an angel and a thin squeaky voice that barely carries across the footlights. When she opens her trap you see that she is a half-wit; when she dances you see that she is a nymphomaniac; when you go to bed with her you see that she is syphilitic.

Last night I went to the Hollywood Restaurant, one of those colossal cabaret entertainments that cost a dollar and a half, *sans vin*, *sans pourboire*. Cold sober you watch a string of dazzling ponies, fifty or more, the finest wenches in the land and empty as a cracked peanut shell. The place is like a huge dance hall, thousands of people eating at once, guzzling it, socking it away. Most of them stone sober and their eyes jumping out of their sockets. Most of them middle-aged, bald, addlepated. They come to hear 'torch songs' sung by middle-aged sirens. Sophie Tucker, the principal event of the evening, sings about a fairy whom she married by mistake. When she says 'Nuts to you!' he answers – 'Oh swish!' She is very fat now, Sophie, and has blue veins relieved by 36 carat rocks. She is advertised as 'the last of the hot mommers.' America isn't breeding any more of this variety. The new ones are perfect – tall, long-waisted, full-busted and rattle-headed. They all sing through the micro-phone, though one could hear just as well without it. There is a deafening roar which, without any wine under your belt, makes you sick and dizzy. They all know how to shout. They love it. They develop whiskey voices – hard, sour, brassy. It goes well with the baby face, the automatic gestures, the broken-hearted lullabys. A colossal show that must cost a fortune and leaves you absolutely unmoved – despite the fine busts I mentioned a while back. I do honestly believe that a poor, skinny, misshapen French woman with just an ounce of personality would stop the show. She would have what the Americans are always talking about but never achieve. She would have *it*. America is minus *it*. You think maybe I'm sour on my own country, but so help me God, that's what's the matter with America – IT. 'They' and 'it' go together – follow me?

And now, Joey, I'm going to tell you a little more about my lonely nights in New York, how I walk up and down Broadway, turning in and out of the side streets, looking into windows and doorways, wondering always when the miracle will happen, and if. And nothing ever happens. The other night I dropped into a lunch counter, a cheesy looking joint on West 45th Street, across the way from the Blue Grotto. A good setting for 'The Killers.' I met some pretty tough eggs, all dressed immaculately, all sallow complexioned and bushy eyebrowed. Faces like sunken craters. The eyes mad and piercing, eyes that pierce right through you and appraise you as so much horse meat. There were a few whores from Sixth Avenue together with some of the most astonishingly beautiful chorus girls I ever laid eyes on. One of these sat next to me. She was so beautiful, so lovely, so fresh, so virginal, so outrageously Palm Olive in every respect that I was ashamed to look her straight in the eye. I looked only at her gloves which were porous and made of fine silk. She had long hair, loose-flowing tresses which hung down almost to her waist. She sat on the high stool and ordered a tiny little sandwich and a container of coffee which she took to her room to nibble at with great delicacy. All the yegg men seemed to know her; they greeted her familiarly but respectfully. She could be 'Miss America, 1935.' She was a dream, I'm telling you. I looked at her furtively through the mirror. I couldn't imagine anyone laying her except he had a golden wand. I couldn't imagine her hoofing it either. I couldn't imagine her eating a big juicy steak with mushrooms and onions. I couldn't imagine her going to the bathroom, unless to clear her throat. I couldn't imagine her having a private life. I can only imagine her posing for a magazine cover, standing perpetually in her Palm Olive skin and never perspiring. I like the gangsters best. These boys go everywhere and by aeroplane and streamlined platinum, lighter than air, air-conditioned trains. They are the only ones in America who are enjoying life, while it lasts. I envy them. I like the shirts they wear, and the bright ties, and the flashy haircuts. They come fresh from the laundry and kill in their best clothes.

The opposite to this is the suburban life. Manhasset, for instance. The idea is – how to kill the weekend. Those who don't play bridge invent other forms of amusement, such as the peep show. Was taken to the cellar of a big advertising director and shown some dirty films. Not a consecutive film, but patches of this and that, *mostly ass*. You see a woman lying on a couch and a man running his hand up her leg; you see her stomach quiver and then another man is standing behind a woman, with his pants down, and he's socking it into her. Then you see a close-up of a cunt – just the cunt – and you watch it open like an oyster to swallow a long slimy penis belonging to a man with a derby. One thing after another, *sans suite*. Afterwards the men go upstairs and maul the women. They like to get undressed and dance over the weekends. To change wives. They don't know what to do with themselves after a hard week at the office. *Donc*, the car, the whiskey bottle, some strange cunt, an artist if possible. (I, for example, made a hit because 'I was so unconventional.' Sometimes, when you are regarded as being so unconventional, it is embarrassing to be obliged to refuse a choice piece of ass – your host's wife, let us say, size 59 and round as a tub. Larry's wife, for example, is a miniature hippopotamus who gets jealous if you dance with any of the good-looking wenches. She goes off and sulks.)

And now let me tell you what one brilliant man in the suburbs thought of last weekend to regale us. When we were all good and crocked he got out an old talking record of the Prince of Wales. We had to listen to that high and mighty potentate (then about nineteen years of age) tell us what the *ideallll* of the Englishman was. I don't have to tell you, Joey, that it was our old friend 'fair play.' An Englishman never *twists* you. No sirree. It went on for three records – it must have been a golden jubilee or something. In the midst of it I got hysterical and began to laugh. I laughed and laughed and laughed. Everybody began to laugh, even the host who, I discovered later, was highly insulted. No sir, an Englishman never *twists* you! He just falls asleep on you…

According to Mlle Bohy, who I agree is a horse's ass, there is no demand here anymore for French literature. She says the Americans are laying off the French. The truth is, she's ashamed of her own country and is trying to become a full-fledged American woman. 'America is a wonderful country for a woman,' she says to me. I thought to myself – Yeah, for a big cow like you who hasn't any more sex appeal… This is the country for woman's rights. This is a matriarchy. A matriarchy of fat old dowagers with whiskers on their chins, a matriarchy of blue noses and flat-breasted heifers. Women are better off in the countries where they are supposedly mistreated.

Last night Jack Brent came to town with his streamlined Packard. He calls me up from his suite at the Albemarle Hotel.

Mr Brent speaking! Ahem! We pick up a cunt on the way and go to Ticino's for dinner. In the front of the basement is a billiard table where the laborers shoot some kind of crazy pool. This lends atmosphere – for the Village artists who frequent the joint.

Anyway, here's how we started the meal – the cunt, Jack and I... We start with six martini cocktails – Brent insists that they be brought all at once. OK. There they are – six of them staring us in the face. Then the menu. Antipasto with steak! Olives and macaroni! While we are lapping up the cocktails Brent orders a few more drinks – to make sure we don't go dry. I venture to suggest wine. He says – *later!* OK. We order three sidecars and two old-fashioneds. A vicious assortment. I'm hungry. It's about 9.30 p.m. Nothing but celery stalks so far. The cocktails make you sick and you talk a lot of drunken shit between whiles. (For instance, a long speech from Brent about a letter I wrote him in 1924 – a letter in which I insulted him, *him*, Jack Brent, the millionaire's son. Now he likes that letter. He shows it around. Proud of it, in fact. He'd like me to insult him some more – that is, if I could do it delicately.)

When the food arrives I demand some wine. I ask for red wine, naturally. Brent doesn't like red wine – says it's no good. Jesus, I'm wondering if there are to be more sidecars, or perhaps some fandangled limousine of a drink. But no, he calls the waiter very ostentatiously, runs down the wine list, and settles on a Graves – *the best!* that is, the highest-priced. It happens to be really good. I leave the cocktails and sidecars to one side and ply the wine. Seeing me drink a big bottle all by myself Brent gets sore. He says he wants to drink some wine also. Good. I pour him out a glass. The cunt only drinks a mouthful and pushes the glass away. She's never had a good glass of wine in her life. Finally I call the waiter over. He's an intelligent dago and he seems to have good taste. I invite him to have a drink with us.

He pours himself out a big tumblerful of the Graves. I can see Brent wincing. He wasn't ordering wine for me to pour it down the waiter's throat. But down it goes. Hurrah! That cheers me up a bit. I like to be friendly with the waiters.

After the steak and radishes, the macaroni and sidecars and gin fizzes and whiskey sours and wine and what not, we have some brandy. Brent wants Napoleon brandy no less. We down the brandy and it's like firewater. We're standing up on our hind legs now, rearing to go. I pullout a five-dollar bill, pretending to split the bill with him, but he pushes it aside. The bill comes to $18.00. Try to imagine what that is – $18.00! Almost a week's wages. And this guy hasn't tasted anything! He's been smoking a cigar all during the meal, and now he's lighting another, and when that's finished he'll light another from the dead end of the last one. Anyhow, we pile into the Packard and start towards Broadway. The lights fizzing just as always and always it looks marvellous – and always it's disappointing once you're in the thick of it. We stop off at a bar en route – to have a little drink before tackling the dance halls. Brent orders in French now. The bartender, a fat mick, looks at him blankly and asks what language he is speaking. Try and order a sidecar in French! Or any hard drink. Well, that down, we descend a few steps to find ourselves in the Silver Slipper where it is advertised that there are nothing but the world's most beautiful show girls as hostesses. There are nothing but hostesses here, half nude, and shivering because of lack of customers. They light up electrically as you enter. It costs only a quarter to *enter*. It costs about $20.00 *to leave*. They advertise 'a nickel a dance,' and it's true enough, but a dance lasts about two minutes, or less. The music never stops – just a little knock-knock when a new tune commences. Waltzing around with a ravishing show girl you don't notice the tunes being knocked off. It's like the click of a taximeter. Suddenly, however, she says: 'Won't you please get another strip of tickets?' A strip costs a dollar which, as I say, you burn up in about eight and a half minutes. Sometimes you sit out a dance while your hostess drinks a Coca-Cola or an orange juice, or perhaps eats a banana layer cake. They are always hungry and thirsty, as you know. *And never drunk.* The law forbids even beer to be sold in these places. The girl is not allowed to sit at the table with you, but only at the railing by your side. She must sit on the railing and lean over to sip her drink. It's a wonder they permit them to smoke – or fuck. The one I picked asked me very innocently what I had come for and I said – 'Why, to get a lay, of course.' Whereupon she pretended to be highly insulted and wanted to walk off. 'Go ahead,' I said. But instead of going she clings to me like a leech.

Well, after I had used up about eight dollars of Brent's money I squandered a couple of my own. Then I got fed up. They are all willing to be laid, but they want a snack first and then a little ride and I suppose after that a little hush money, and with this and that, a little here and a little there, and here a little and there a little, why the dawn would be breaking just about the time you'd be trying to pull their pants off.

When we got outside we forgot where we had parked the car. You have to park blocks away from Broadway – there are so many cars lined up. We wandered around stupidly, up and down side streets, looking for Brent's streamlined Packard. We found it finally and just as we were about to pile in along comes a tough bimbo who sails up to two janes standing against a railing. Without a word he hauls off and socks one of them in the jaw. Then he snatches the bag from her hand and dumps the contents into the gutter. He gives her another crack for good measure and walks off. By this time I had already climbed into the car. I felt nervous and uneasy. Brent, however, like a chevalier, bends down and picks up the money lying in the street. Then, in his best manner, he goes up to the girl and handing her the dough, he says: 'Lady, would you like me to take a sock at that guy for you? I will, if you say so.' The guy, by the way, is almost out of sight now. Anyway, the 'lady' makes a grab for the dough, counts it quickly, and then yells – 'Hey, what do you mean holding out on me like that? Where's the other dollar?' With that Brent climbs into the car, starts the motor, and then just as he's giving her the gas, he leans out of the window and says – in his best manner – 'Lady, go fuck yourself!' and we drive off.

Well, that's the third most interesting night I've had since I'm here, so you can imagine what the rest must be like. The other two I forget already, but I know there were three. Joe has just taken me to lunch; we sat three hours or more, talking about the old days when we hiked through the South together. He was just telling me about the time I was hustled out of the railroad station in Jacksonville at the point of a gun – an incident I had almost completely forgotten. But the thing I do remember vividly – and I will remember it all my life – is that whack over the ass I got when I was sleeping on a bench in the park, at Jacksonville. That I shall never forgive the city of Jacksonville! I will put it down in every book I write – with variations. My ass is still smarting!

Well, these reminiscences only serve to remind me to tell you that everything is just the same here and that I would still be leading a dog's life if I had to depend on America for inspiration. The reason I write you this long letter is because for ten days now I have been unable to write a line. New York crushes you. You can't breathe. It's not the noise and dust, nor the traffic, nor the crowds – it's the appalling flatness, ugliness, monotony and sameness of everything. The walls bear down on you. One wall is like another, and there are no advertisements of Pernod Fils or Amer Picon or Suze or Marie Brizard or Zigzag. The walls are bare and, in the case of the skyscrapers, they are like huge railroad tracks standing up, gleaming, metallic, straight as a die – walls broken only by millions of windows which are let up here and there like organ stops. As you come within range of a sky-scraper you get caught up in a maelstrom. The wind eddies about the base of the building and almost lifts you off your feet. You stand and gape at these buildings night after night, half amused, half disgusted, half awed, and you say '*our* this,' and '*our* that,' and then you go to a cafeteria and order a ham sandwich with a cup of weak coffee and think what a grand time you didn't have.

I told you that I intended writing a final section to the book, to be called – 'I the Human Being.' Well, I wrote about six pages and had to quit. I feel that I am no longer a human being. I am just a biped, an animal what eats and sleeps – *its* and *slips*, as the Mocks say. 'I slips well,' you hear on the street. Or a guy says to a woman in broad daylight, corner of 45th Street and Broadway: 'Now I tell you what to do, Rose... Saturday you go home and you give yourself a thorough cleaning out.' Just like that! *Alors*, who goes there, *friend or enema*?

The other day I ventured a visit to the Radio City Theatre. Joe slept soundly throughout the performance. Maybe I told you about this before – about the giant octopi that float on a gauze screen while three thousand chorines dance the *Liebestraum* a mile off? Everything colossal. Colossally colossal. The theatre itself magnificent – the last word in modern architecture. As soon as you cough it is ventilated – automatically. By thermostat. An average mean temperature of 72 degrees Fahrenheit, winter, spring or summer. No smoking. No smoking anywhere, except in the burlesque. The best you can do is to fart. And, as I said before, even that is immediately cleared off by thermostat device... In the lobby there is a piece of mosaic done by somebody or other in which the Muses are depicted. They have added three or four new ones to the original Nine, among them one to Engineering, one to Health, and one to Publicity. Believe it or not, beloved. Every morning, at half past nine punkt, the same radio announcer announces the same wonderful fishing tackle sold in Newark, N.J., by a rodman who makes bamboo poles and just the right tackle with a handsome trawler free of charge just cut out the coupon in the Ladies' Home Journal page 24 last column and don't forget the telephone number is Weehawken 238745 courtesy of the Genuine Diamond Watch Company are you listening the gong is just about to strike the half-hour it is now exactly nine-thirty Eastern Standard Daylight Time.

Well, tomorrow I make application for my passport, and where it says – 'Why do you intend to visit France?' – I shall put down as I did the last time – *for pleasure!* Or maybe I'll put down: 'Because I want to become a human being again.' How's that? I am hoping to begin my next book on the boat. It will begin with my life in New York eight or nine years ago, starting off with the Orpheum Dance Palace the night I had 75 bucks in my pocket for the first time in my life and decided I would take a chance and took it. I am going to write this so simply and honestly that my grandchildren, if I have any, will be able to appreciate it. A long, long story and I intend to put in every detail. I've got the rest of my life ahead of me.

Coming by the Champlain, unless I advise you otherwise. Haven't earned a penny, haven't gotten a stick of recognition. This is the grandest country God ever made. Especially the Grand Canyon. One of the greatest blessings ever showered upon mankind is Horlick's Frosted Milk Chocolate. *Or*, the beautiful Men's Room in the Pennsylvania Depot.

Am I happy to leave? No, not happy – *delirious!* From now on it'll be all 13th Arrondissement!

This is one of those incredible New York days when you stay in because you're broke and it's raining. If you're a lucky guy like me you have your friend Joe O'Regan stay with you and make watercolors while you fret and fume. The thing is, when you're in America, you must always obey the law. Take the Conroy Bottle Breaking Machine, for example. This machine, sold at the nominal cost of $125.00 f.o.b. docks or warehouse, enables you to keep within the law and at the same time avoid the risk of cutting your wrist. It breaks empty liquor bottles by a simple movement of the lever on top: thus, if your premises should be raided by Federal Agents all your bottles will be found perfectly broken in accordance with the last idiotic law and you will be spared the penalty of a heavy fine or a year in the penitentiary. Next door to the Conroy Bottle Breaking Machine Co. is the Suke-Yaki restaurant which offers Japanese food at 65¢ per head. You can have your shoes shined outside the restaurant by a nigger who advocates world peace. He advertises it – 'World Peace' – on his shoe box. No extra charge for the shine.

A little further down is the 'Poets' Corner,' a dingy Village rendezvous where the Communist poets sit and chew the fat over a cup of pale, greasy coffee. Here is where America's great poems are made. They are sold a little further up the street for ten cents a piece. You can read them before you buy them as they are all conveniently tacked on to the fence, corner of Washington Square and Thompson Street. Most of them are written in lead pencil and signed by the author who scratches himself while you read. 'Please buy a poem!' he says in a cheery voice. 'Only ten cents the poem!' If it rains of course there is no market. Then you must go directly to the Poets' Corner, downstairs in the basement, a few doors below June Mansfield's[5] old hangout on Third Street – where the 'young and evil' used to congregate. The painters, I must say, are a little better off. They fetch thirty-five and fifty, even seventy cents, for an oil. They are not afraid of the rain because, as you know, oil and water don't mix.

So you think I am shitting you about all this? You ask about the fancy prices paid by *Esquire* and *Vanity Fair*, etc. Well, ask! No poet ever gets into *Vanity Fair* or *Esquire*. These organs are reserved exclusively for he-men like Hemingway and Joe Schrank.[6] They are magazines for MEN. Another thing about these magazines is the wonderful pipeline system leading to the affiliated organs such as *Harper's*, *Vogue*, *Atlantic Monthly*, etc., etc. It's like boarding an open trolley and getting a transfer. *Or* like passing from one wet dream to another and waking utterly refreshed. All this has a bearing on what I am about to tell you – that is, about the treatment of snakes. You see, Joe O'Regan was a snake-fancier, as a boy. He lived with old man Moncure down in Virginia somewhere. Joe was telling me about this as we sat in McElroy's Saloon on Thirty-First Street where, after midnight, you can dance with some of the finest sots ever imported from Ireland. Across the street from McElroy's is the Hebrew National Restaurant where you may see an enlarged photograph of a dinner given by Lou Siegel to his playmates Eddie Cantor, George Jessel, Al Jolson and the other well-known comedians of Jewish vintage. This, for your information, is just opposite the Hotel Wolcott now made famous by my chapter called 'The Tailor Shop,' in memory of my old man and his defunct cronies – Corse Payton, Julian L'Estrange, Tom Ogden, Chucky Morton, et alia. The effect passing the Wolcott and looking over towards the Hebrew National where Eddie Cantor somewhat enlarged makes googoo eyes at George Jessel is nothing less than horripilating. This is what has happened to good old Thirty-First Street in the space of a generation.

But, as I say, Joe and I were talking about scallops. There were a few empty scallop shells on my writing table when we pulled in last night. We pulled in rather broke and disheartened – had to while away the time watching a dance across the way, at the Carroll Club. The Carroll Club is a lovely mansion for poor working girls. On Saturday nights the Settlement workers throw a dance; fashionable young men from West End Avenue and the Bronx drive up in fresh-painted limousines and neck the girls behind the translucent screens which we look down upon from the 23rd story of our little apartment house. The poverty of New York is on a grand scale, as is everything else. Behind this dire poverty stand the hope and courage of 120,000,000 morons and idiots tattooed with the N.R.A. double eagle.[7] Behind this stand the empty bottles which the Conroy Bottle Breaking Machine will break for you at no less than ordinary ground burial. Behind this stands the red Indian who was so despoiled and deprived of all rights that today he is bored with his huge estates and oil wells and clamoring to be treated like a white man.

It was raining, as I say, and Joe and I were standing at Whelan's Cigar Store watching other people watch us. This is at the L station corner of 33rd Street, Sixth Avenue and Broadway. Under the elevated stood a strange figure – a slim young man in dungarees and blue silk shirt with a red bandanna around his neck and a huge sombrero on his bean, rakishly set, of course. He seemed to be waiting for the rain to stop. We had about 75 cents between us, Joe and I, and we didn't know whether to engage the young cowboy in talk or not. Finally we whistled to him and he came over, looking rather startled and apprehensive. He had overslept, he said, and so he had just come down from Holyoke, Mass., where the circus was, and he was training spitz dogs or something. He had a pair of big iron spurs in his pocket which he showed us rather proudly. The rowels were rather dull, but he said they could be sharpened easily. He said he was looking for the Grand Central Depot, in order to find the Travellers' Aid Society. Said it was the biggest taown he had ever been in – just as though there might be dozens of other big towns in the world, even bigger. We asked him how he liked New York. Said he couldn't say cause he had only been in it a half hour and was looking how to get out of it. We took him to the Mills Hotel, paid his fare for the night, and gave I him instructions as to how to get to the ferry in the morning.

After we left him it struck me that this was the most interesting experience I had had since being here. A fine upstanding youth they say, with soft, winsome talk, a dumb animal that had strayed from the fold. All New York owned and run by pushing, grabbing Jews: a frozen clatter over your head day and night; grim, overweening buildings pushing you back into the concrete; the lights blinking like mad, red to stop, green to go; suits in every window, and an extra pair of trousers, if you choose – *Sanforized* too, whatever the hell that means. I remember how we took his ten-gallon hat, how we felt it, weighed it, rolled it, crumpled it, tried it on, looked at the label, asked the price of it, etc., etc. That man and that hat were worth more to me than all New York put together – I mean the whole damned city and what it stands for... even with cellophane around it. Here was one of our own kind, a dumb animal lost and stray walking in the rain, zigzagging under the L, ducking taxis, his blue shirt open at the chest, his hair wet and glistening, trim figure, nineteen years old, muscles of steel, eyes like a deer, horny hands, blue dungarees, the pockets cut on the bias. Strike me dead if I didn't envy him! He was heading back to Tennessee, where it would be all farm and no more circus. In the morning the bums will wean him his last few pennies and he will stand on a corner looking helplessly for the ferry we told him to take. His name was Self. Will Self. I want you to remember that. It's a swell American name, good in any language. Reminds me distantly of 'The Ego and His Own,'[8] a fat, pretentious piece of anarchism which I read in Chula Vista when I was trying hard to be a cowboy myself – only the bedbugs wouldn't let me.

So, as we were sitting in McElroy's Saloon Joe started to reminisce – about Miami and the great tornado of 1927 or '8, just after the boom. He's talking to me about a wench he had on the beach under a row boat, during the cyclone. Just as he's a-straddle of her along come the Miami gallon-nippers (a species of exaggerated mosquito) and they start nipping him in the ass. From this to the sunrise in Key West and the shapes of the clouds, one back of another, big, balloonlike, some like Buffalo Bill, some like Sitting Bull, and all in violent colors. We're standing under an arc light in St Petersburg – the old men's retreat – and suddenly the mosquitos are biting us, millions and millions of them. We're playing a nineteen-hole game of golf on the run, with the mosquitos chasing us. And then the clear springs which come up out of nowhere, the fish eating out of your hand through the glass-bottomed boats. (Does this remind you a little of Blaise Cendrars?[9]) Better still… when you dig a hole to drain off the water the water disappears and nobody knows where to. The St. Johns River is the only river in the United States which runs from south to north, i.e., uphill. Hence Ponce de Leon…[10]

But it was with old Moncure, when they came up north to Madison Square Garden, that Joe found out about snakes. They were travelling with the carnival then. Joe says, and I take it on his authority, that snakes have been so molested from time immemorial that when they are treated with a little tenderness they respond very warmly. What Joe used to do was to run a king snake up his left sleeve, across the back of his vest, and down through the right sleeve – in order to feed it a raw egg. (I asked if it was customary to peel the egg first, but Joe says no.) Anyway, the king snake knows whether an egg is good or not. You can't give him a bad egg. He's clean, the snake. Eats no garbage, as do the heathen Chinese. No sirree. Once in a while he resorts to cannibalism, but he must be very hungry first. The thing to do, when he gets this way, is to put a younger king snake – a snake *cadet* – in the same cell with him. Don't put a rat in as the rat is apt to kill the snake. What Joe used to do was to wait for the big snake to gobble the little one. When the jaws were firmly locked about the little snake's neck Joe would get out his jackknife and, making a ring around the little snake's neck, he would let the big snake hold while he pulled off the little snake's skin. When you feed the snake a raw egg, you must cup the egg with your five fingers. This endears the snake to you, or you to him. When the snake has swallowed the egg he spits out the shell. This, I think, is the most wonderful part of the egg story. Imagine what a feat this is! First swallowing the egg whole, then crushing it, then digesting it, then spitting out the shell. I think any man who sincerely wanted to make friends with a snake should also go to the trouble of shelling the egg for the snake. Or parboiling it, at least. There are little delicacies which even a snake can learn to appreciate. More especially since the snake has no way of thanking you, except by rolling his eyes.

You see, I am having a very interesting time in New York. Like the other day, for example, when I revisited the scene of my childhood – at Paradise Point. We had to go there and back, eat, gas up, turn around and take a shower, all in five and a half hours. It's a little over a hundred miles to Paradise Point. All I had time for was a quick look at the bay – Peconic Bay, say OK, void a little urine, pick up some dead crabs, and tumble back into the rumble seat. That's how things are done in America. Even sacred things, such as exploring Swann's Way. There I was, a hundred-per-cent Proust, remembering everything in advance, getting all tremulous and sweaty, and suddenly we're there – that's it! – and bango, like a streak we're off again. Here is where I offer a new point of view on memory and childhood. The strange thing about this little excursion is this – the place looked even better to me after a lapse of 35 years than before! This must be one of those places which obey the Fraenkelian law – they live back ever more beautiful, ever more wondrous. They grow younger with time. When I was a kid it was just Peconic Bay to me, plus a few pretty sea shells. Yesterday, or the day before, it was Capri, the Mediterranean, Majorca, Cyprus, what have you. The miracle is that nobody comes here. The Jews have left it undiscovered. Not one more house than thirty-five years ago. Not one more inhabitant. Not one more duck farm, or any other kind of farm. Something rare and strange about this. Especially in America where things grow so fast and so large over night.

(Interruption: Joe is so excited over his watercolor that he is painting on his knees. We have only one piece of paper left and he is slaving in the margin. He is doing a corner of my room which I will send you by second-class mail.)

And now, before leaving the subject of Paradise Point, I want to answer a question you posed about my shit – any blood, etc.? We were talking about that this morning, Joe and I, on our way to the drugstore for breakfast. Joe says one should never concentrate on one's stool. One should forget about it. The Formosans, he says, sometimes go three and four days without crapping. When they get ready to crap they crap. They do it by simply constricting the bowels, as Joe explains it. It is unnecessary to go to the toilet regularly, he adds. What is not passed out immediately is absorbed by the system. The system requires it, or ergo, it would have been evacuated. This is a kind of logic which I respect, which I can cope with. It makes me feel better at once. Not that I am troubled with constipation. No, my trouble is a slit, or vent, in the anal passage, due to the delicacy of the membranes. After visiting Doctor Larsen and having him stipple my arteries with a stippler I have no trouble whatever, neither loss of blood, neither dizziness. But I must visit him every six months or so to be restippled. Eventually I will have a sort of stucco interior, I suppose. Bloodproof and fireproof.

Joe has just finished the watercolor of a corner of the room. He says it is a little out of perspective. It is also a little fraudulent, as he has not reproduced my picture of the womb very well. He has substituted a flowerpot with blue cornflowers. He says he doesn't like to do wombs – they make him nervous. I had this womb framed, you know. Didn't know I had done a womb until Doctor Larsen came along and explained it to me. I thought I was doing a self-portrait, or had done it. But no, Doctor Larsen points out the horns of the womb and adds – 'You must have copied it from my old anatomy book.' Larsen is the sort of chap who sees everything in scientific terms. If we go to a German restaurant he shows his tactfulness by talking about a pocketful of cyanide, how just a pocketful would kill off Hitler and his whole crowd. This is just the thing to put us in good grace with the waiter.

Interruption of several hours during which we walked our legs off trying to 'find a friendly face,' someone who would lend us a quart or a half dollar for a meal. In this land there are no empty wine bottles to cash in. When you are broke here you may as well go out and hang yourself. And now, with a slightly drawn belly I am going to tell you a little more about America…

I am thinking how good it is to be on the earth and just healthy, to have a fine appetite and all your teeth. If ever I come back to this country I will skip New York and go straight to the sticks where there are nothing but ignorant and adorable people. The intellectuals are in my hair – and the artists and the Communists and the Jews. New York is an aquarium – maybe I said this before – where there are nothing but hellbenders and lungfish and slimy, snag-toothed groupers and sharks with pilot fish aft and stern. You look through the glass casing and you see the bloated monsters sailing by. Now and then you see a Rudd, or a Johnny Darter, or maybe a whiting. Now and then a clownfish. But mostly it's hellbenders and slugs and the slippery, slimy, green moray that winds through the crevices of the rocks and licks its own tail. When you go to Stewart's Cafeteria you see them coming in on crutches, infantile paralysis cases that eat like a man rowing a boat. Big Jewfish with moon-faced mouths that swallow whole cabbages and the dried vomit which is offered gratis on the free snack counter. Passing through 31st Street you see the National Jewish Book Concern, with titles such as these: 'What Danny Did': stories for the wee Jewish child. Or 'Modern Kosher Meals': menus according to the Jewish dietary laws. Or 'The Ghetto Messenger' – showing Sol Slivovitz delivering Western Union messages on the East Side. Or 'Cohen Comes First.' Or 'Why I Am a Jew' – by a Jew. Or 'The City Without Jews' – *show me it!* Or, Harry Hershfield's Jewish Jokes – culled at Ye Olde Salami Shoppe.

And this brings me to Seidler's Beach... It was like this... All day we had been in the country, eating and drinking, at Mr Richard's little farm. Mr Richard is a Gentile whom Boris and Cronstadt made a point of contact with. That is to say, in order to flop on Mr Richard's lawn and picnic there they had to pretend to Mr Richard that they were thinking of buying his farm and would he be able to vacate the premises in ten days let us say. Anyway, when evening came on we started down the hill towards the ocean. I hadn't the faintest idea where we were and I didn't care. I remember passing New Brunswick and in a half-drunken stupor admiring its pseudomediaeval glamour. The next thing I remember is Seidler's Beach and a big casino with not a soul inside. And there is the Atlantic Ocean – miles and miles of it! It's night now and I'm walking up and down the boardwalk to get the intellectualism out of my hair. It's like this, Joey... All afternoon they had been plaguing me with 'race logic,' a new theme that Boris had developed since his return from Alaska. The idea is – to go mad. All afternoon he's whining because I don't go mad in life, but only in my writing. I say I don't want to go mad – yet. He says I must learn to live alone and apart. I say 'not yet.' Then we all fall asleep racing through Red Bank, Skeonk and points east. We stop short in front of a telegraph pole and get out to take a leak. Here there is a charming old couple who run a little booth with pop soda and whatnot. We bring the whiskey bottles out and order ice and seltzer water. The old woman, a half-wit by the way, says she is not afraid to die only she 'wants to be taken quick.' This appeals to Boris so much that we are delayed in getting to Seidler's Beach. Nobody knows why Seidler's Beach: it's on the program, that's all. The old couple are very soothing to the nerves in their half-witted way; they bring us aspirin and Bromo-Seltzer which we mix with the whiskey and soda. What I am trying to tell you, Joey, is how fine it is to get out and stand under the stars, to shake the cobwebs out of your hair, to hear nothing, to smell saltwater, to nibble at a whiting. Very tonic and refreshing – coming after the 'race logic.'

The casino at Seidler's Beach is clean as a hound's tooth. It is also very clear that we are not wanted – *moi non plus, parce que avec ces gens-là pourquoi pas. On me prend pour un sale juif aussi.*[11] You follow me? I notice the cold shoulder all right, but to pass it off I put a nickel in the slot and while the music plays I walk nonchalantly towards the boardwalk breathing deep breaths of the ocean air. I leave it to the others to order the spread. In order to show that they are well travelled they order three bottles of Macon – the real stuff – and when it comes chilled to the table they send it back and order it warmed up a bit. Then they inquire about the food, whether it is good or not, because they want only the very best. And they must know the waitress's name. That settled, Cronstadt in his playful way introduces himself as a poet, Boris as a publisher, and I'm also supposed to be somebody but I don't listen, or I pretend not to hear, not wishing to be confounded with publishers and poets of this stripe. The meal is a mixture of race logic and red cabbage. Jeans & Eddington[12] are served cold with a little fried snot on the side. Spengler[13] is chilled to the temperature of the room. Boris is talking about race logic and contacts. Cronstadt is laughing so hard that the tears are rolling down his face. I don't know why they're laughing so. I can see the waitress glowering at us: I know we're not wanted. Suddenly Jill remembers that she hadn't piddled since we were at Mr Richard's place, so she goes out on the beach and squats in the sand. Outside it is starlight and the sloops and frigates are at anchor, together with the oyster dredges and the submarine chasers. I can't believe that there are three bottles of Macon in front of me. With these friendly bottles staring me in the face I ought to be in France; instead, I am with three crazy Jews who are talking race logic and red cabbage. Supposing now I had been with three Gentiles – say Emil Schnellock, Joe O'Regan and Bill Dewar. And supposing we had all passed the grammar school test safely. Do you suppose that with three bottles of Macon in front of us and the breakers roaring outside in the starlight that we would be pissing the night away on race logic and red cabbage? Not I! I imagine that by this time we would be singing, and maybe a little later going out to look at the stars. I imagine that if we had been three Gentiles there would have been a wall of clams three feet high all along the ocean front and each clam singing to us with a broken heart. I imagine the best and the worst, *but not race logic*.

Are you getting a good clear picture of America? If not, I'll wipe the lens off. Stand back a little now and listen to this…

Back of New York City there is a vast landscape which stretches to the Pacific. The man who owns it is a chain store called the Atlantic and Pacific Tea Company. They employ only Irish help, and they must be green at that. All along the Lincoln Highway there are booths with hot dogs inside. You gas up every hundred miles or so, according to the nature of your car. When you come to Albuquerque you run into mesquite and sagebrush; there are mesas and tablelands and fresh spinach if you so desire it. These come from the truck farms in Imperial Valley, along with bumper melons and clusters of wild grapes. At night you listen to the coyotes; in the morning it's factory bells and the chain gang. On either side of the Mississippi, which is directly down the center of the United States, are the buffalo ranges where cowboys in silk shirts and ten-gallon hats sing hill-billy songs at twilight – for the radio. Further south you strike the Ozarks, in the midst of which is Mena the Labor College. When you come to Utah you take your clothes off and float in the Salt Sea. You bob up and down for a while and then you strike due west for the Mojave Desert where it is all moonlight and cactus. Now and then you pass the ghost of a buffalo, or the twenty-mule team bringing in the borax. At Needles you get out and boil an egg in the sand. Then you slip back to Yuma, because it's a nice name, and you shiver. Finally you come to Imperial City which flourished in the old Roman days, vestiges of which may still be seen by the tourist who gets off the beaten track along the ivy-colored walls that form the ramparts of the old city said by some to have been founded even before the Romans, by the descendants of the lost continent of Mu, pro-nounced Mieux. Relics of this lost race can still be traced in the city of Tulsa, due to the digging of oil wells and small privies. The true Tulsan still speaks with a click-clack, as in days of yore.

(I'm still hoping that some one will call up and invite me out to dinner. It's only 1.30 a.m. now.)

Time presses and the Veendam doesn't sail till Friday. I have an upper berth and share my stateroom with three other gentlemen. If they are American it will be all right; if they are Dutch it will be just too bad. But the Dutch breakfast is good, I am told, and I shall be up early every morning waiting for the bell to ring. There are now twelve men and a woman in New York City who know that I am a genius. So Cronstadt informs me. A genius must eat and drink: I hope these twelve men and a woman will remember that. And I hope you will have a good spread waiting for me when I land. I would like to go back to the Villa Seurat immediately and sit down to the table right now. Tomorrow it will be too late. Tomorrow I will have eaten already. Now I am hungry, and by Christ, if to be a saint means to be hungry, then I am going to stop being a saint. There was a man died the other day – of starvation. Seems he had two stomachs, and it was too big a job keeping them both filled. It got beyond him. Also a woman who had a stomach upside down; after they righted it for her she went on a roller coaster to test it out. *I have one small stomach which is getting smaller and smaller. I hope I have just enough genius to keep it filled regularly, and nothing more.* I hope to sit down soon to a dish of squangeels, which is an American offshore dinner composed of snails, scallops, oysters, clams, shrimps, lamb fries, bread crumbs, garlic, liverwurst, sauerbraten, onions, romaine salad, black olives, celery stalks, asparagus tips, watermelon rinds, sauerkraut, chopped chicken livers, pigeon eggs, sweetbreads, sausage, the white of an egg and a slather of mustard.

A genius should not be allowed to starve completely. He should be half-starved, or three-quarters starved. He needs only a little nourishment to fill out the tucks in his breadbasket, but he needs that little badly. Just now it's nip and tuck. I feel like an old scow after it's been reamed and caulked. I feel as though I were still good for many a voyage, but I'm bleached and drying in the sun now. They say one gets mystical when he is hungry and starved – but I get practical and cunning. I got so sly and cunning a few moments ago that I went downstairs and borrowed a quarter from the bellhop. I asked for a quarter and he handed me a dollar. That shows what a genius I am! And now, Joey, I don't want you to feel badly about this because when you read this I shall be on the high seas where it is all Dutch breakfast and Holland gin. I shall be walking the poop deck between snacks, and I am positive there will be some bore walking beside me and telling me the story of his life. I was in hopes of starting my next book aboard the boat but I am afraid to bring the typewriter along for fear they will make me pay duty on it. Anyway, I have started it in my head. I know the whole thing, from beginning to end. And this time I feel sure it will pour out of me like wine from the bunghole. I have a plan of writing concentrically, which will allow me the utmost freedom while still preserving the illusion of motion and progress. I shall travel light and ship all baggage ahead, by American Express. That means overboard with analysis and introspection, overboard with race logic and surrealism, overboard with form and style. This story I have to tell is so human that even a dog could tell it. I being just a notch above the dog in lingual ability will of course take a little longer to tell it – but it's the same story. It's the story of being alone on the earth and hungry most of the time, hungry not for food and sex merely, but for everything. I am looking out of a porthole on my life which is running parallel to me and slowly sinking, like a four-masted schooner in a gale. I will let everybody have his own say and take his own sweet time about it. I expect to eat and sleep in the book, and when I want to take a leak I'll take it – right in the book. I thought it all out one night walking up and down Broadway in the crowd. There was such a crowd milling about me that suddenly I realized that I was quite alone and I got to like the feeling of being rubbed by strange elbows and jostled and shoved and stepped on and spat on, etc., etc. I saw the opening chapter very quietly, as if suddenly all the noise had stopped and there was just one big green light – To Go! – and it was shining on my book. That was the signal to go ahead, and I went ahead full steam. I could recall anything I chose to recall – and with all the filaments and tendrils attached. All I have to do now is to start in, to say – 'Hello! here we are... how are you!' The rest follows as a matter of course. It is the story of my life, to which I find there is no end. The miracle is that one should ever want to write about anybody else. One's life! A whirlpool with a hole in the center. Just as you are writing the last page you get sucked under – and there's your *one's life* for you! Well, I am going down with my own life – and let nobody try to throw me a life preserver. *Throw me a few meals now!* And put a little gravy on the potatoes. Even a genius likes gravy with his meat. I don't say Worcestershire Sauce or Yorkshire pudding – just a bit of black gravy, slightly sour, and if you have a spare Kartoffelklösse[14] throw that in with the gravy. (Did I spell Kartoffelklösse right this time? Never mind the umlauts – they will come later. Now is the time for dumplings and black gravy.)

The Maison Gerard is an old-world restaurant on 33rd Street just opposite the Post Office. The inside is somewhat like a lunatic asylum, only *mignon*.[15] Everything is *mignon*, including the spittoons. Everything has been spat on and polished with a greasy rag. In the rear of the restaurant is an old-world garden fitted up with swings, scups, hammocks, ping-pong tables, rockers, Morris chairs and whatever bric-a-brac it was impossible to squeeze into the salon. Everything in the worst taste, but adorably *mignon*. Monsieur Gerard himself escorted me through the establishment – in case I should be looking for a pension on my next visit to America. As I say, the Maison Gerard has a little of that warm, cosy, attractive quality of the lunatic asylum. There are saucers from a bistrot in Ménilmontant, umbrellas from last year, a Singer Sewing Machine, a Haynes piano, model 1903, hassocks for the cats, and so on. The food is crazy too – even crazier than the toilet which has just been renovated. It's just the place to come, on a cold winter's day, and settle down to read *Voyage au Bout de la Nuit*.[16] Madame Gerard, the patron's wife, resembles Madame Bonat of the Maison Bonat on 31st Street, same latitude and longitude. That is to say, they are both cripples and waddle a bit. They are both peppery and mercenary, with that pleasant, artificial smile of the storekeeper who knows his onions. Immediately they stop talking the smile goes out like an electric light. It is the smile of French commerce, *and I love it*.

Walking up Eighth Avenue after dinner I recapture that impression of the city which I had one day standing on the roof of the Empire State Building. This section of the city is taken from *Metropolis* – I mean it is a little out of date already. Millions and millions of windows, toy blocks that fit one inside the other, like a movie setting. It's only when you get up on top of a skyscraper that you can see the humus of old buildings out of which this fantastic toy block world has been created. Looking down on the low roofs of the dingy red-brick buildings you might well imagine that New York was an island over which there flew endless flocks of obscene migratory birds. The whole city seems to be covered with bird lime. Everything old has a portico and Corinthian columns. The Catholic churches, such as St. Anthony's, for instance, look like the dregs of a dragged out novena: all front and mustache, with mourners marching up the steps towards the altar. The synagogues look like Turkish baths; they are usually abandoned Lutheran churches with stained-glass windows. I have been doing a lot of walking about the fish markets and morgues and asylums. I like the waterfront hospitals, all equipped with sun terraces mounted on iron scaffolds that remind you vaguely of the dreams of Mantegna. Only these are fireproof dreams.

And now I am going to tell you how a genius finds recreation in a city like New York. You walk north until you come to 42nd Street which has now become a public shithouse. Five burlesque houses in one block, and all of them Jewish, even the black-and-tan. In between are sandwich joints, penny arcades and movies at fifteen cents a crack. Special fifteen-cent movies with fifteen-cent actors and actresses, all low-grade morons with clean hearts who look you straight in the eye. A continuous performance from eight in the morning to midnight; it slides before your eyes like a tide of shit. All these movie houses were once good theatres; now they are filled with chinks, wops, polaks, litvaks, mocks, croats, finns, etc. Now and then a half-witted hundred-percent American from Gallup or Terre Haute. In the toilet I read this: 'Kill Hitler and save the Mocks. Join the Jewish Navy and ship pork to Jerusalem.' Beneath it was an advertisement by the Wrigley Brothers, the last line of which read: '*The finest gum since the dawn of time.*'

Coming away from one of these joints the other night I bumped into Jack Kweller of Brighton Beach. Jack Kweller was one of my Western Union messengers in the old days. He has become even more monstrously fat than before and was fitted out with a peak cap advertising a cheap dance hall. A puller-in, in other words. When I told him I had been in Paris all these years he said immediately – 'Do you know Henri Barbusse?'[17] I had to confess that I didn't know Henri Barbusse personally. He seemed to be surprised at this. Said he had gotten acquainted with Barbusse at the John Reed Club. He began at once to talk about Anthropology, the Woman Question, Race Suicide,

Prostitution, Marxian Dialectics, and so on and so forth. Since quitting the Western Union he had put his time to good account, he said. Up until the crisis he had been making toys. I thought of the innocent Jack Kweller I knew in the days when the Olympic burlesque flourished at Tammany Hall. Kweller was an usher then and he used to give me a seat up front for a little tip. Then one day he took me aside and begged me to give him a messenger boy's job, which I did. And a very good messenger he turned out to be. He used to work the night shift – seven days a week, twelve hours a day, at $17.50 a week flat. On this he managed to lay aside a little nest egg so as to take up toy making. After he had become expert at his job he started reading up on Anthropology, Ethnology, Political Science, Sociology, Economics, etc., all those useless subjects which advance one in life – *barring a crisis*. All *Jewish* subjects, I might add. The ambition of every industrious, self-respecting Jew is to become a member of the School for Social Science, or the John Reed Club, or the Rand School, or better still, all three at once. This gives him a knowledge of the world, keeps him *au courant*, with hot and cold water always on tap – get me? When he goes to the Automat to save ten cents he always has a book with him and while standing up like a horse in the manger he munches his political science along with the stale bread and the tomato ketchup. A Jew can read a fat book while walking the street, especially if it is a learned work, and all learned works are thick and fat, as you know.

Well, anyway, as I was taking leave of Jack Kweller he gave me his personal card so that I might go to the Bann Box and sit down and have a cheap drink for sixty-five cents or so and perhaps find a Ziegfield Follies beauty to dance with. The Bann Box is a little joint over a stable on one of the dark side streets. Once you get in it's hard to get out. I knew when I entered the joint that I didn't have enough money to sit down and hire a dance partner. But I like to walk in and look at these joints. To make it short, I walked in brisk and dapper, looking my alertest(!) and, going up to the bartender, I asked very innocently if he could tell me what had become of my old friend Jack Kweller. The bartender referred me to a tough mug who was the bouncer, I guess. I looked as though I might have money so it was easy to keep a straight face. I asked again about my old friend Jack Kweller. Said I had been away about ten years, been up to Alaska and all that shit. I said I had a message for Jack from one of his pals up there, a placer-miner he was. Of course I was promptly informed that Jack could be found standing outside the dance hall. I thanked him very cordially and promised to get hold of Jack and bring him back with me as soon as he was off duty. The bouncer said that would be fine and with that he takes me by the arm, escorts me to the bar, and orders a drink on the house. I fished around for my wallet as though I couldn't stand for a thing like that, but he wouldn't listen to me. Then I asked if he wouldn't have a drink with me, but fortunately someone just walked in and he had to refuse hastily. If he had accepted I would have been shit out of luck. I probably would have gone to the toilet and tried to beat it out the back way or something. Anyway, Joey, this is where a little front and mustachio comes in handy. Always look the part! Look 'em straight in the eye and be innocent! Always say you've been to Alaska, or Tahiti. I said Alaska because I wasn't sunburned enough to have been in Tahiti ten years. That was quick thinking for me, *for a Goy*, what I mean.

Walking down Broadway I noticed how lousy the street was with whores. Not the old bag-swingers of 1908 and '10, but young ones without stockings, lean, trim, racy ones with strips of monkey fur or skunk slung around their necks. They come bouncing out of the side streets with a cigarette to their lips and they stand a moment looking bewilderedly up and down the

Appian Way. They look right through you, not graciously and invitingly and sexually and sensually, but with that boring, riveting eye like the acetylene torch on the car tracks at night. There is only one look the American woman can turn on, be she a whore or a duchess. European women have a thousand looks. The American gal has just one. And that's a searchlight which sprays your spine and throws no heat. It speaks of cold cash and speed and sanitary conditions. Drunk or sober, it's the same thing. It's not sex, but the light of a powerful apparatus hidden in the hind lobe of the brain, just above the medulla oblongata. It's like a music box in which you drop a coin, like a chewing gum slot machine, like a London gas meter. You drop the coin, the jiggers start, there's a little flirr and movement, a whirr and then the light goes on, stays on just long enough to read what's written and is off again. Don't think they come up to you and solicit you. Ah no! They stand there in the gloom of a stage exit and suddenly, when they espy you, they leap forward, matching your stride with theirs, moving in closer and closer, always parallel and abreast of you, until your arms touch, and then your hips, and when you have rubbed each other well, like a couple of old alley cats, they let you open your trap and make a price, still walking, still nonchalant, blasé, indifferent, cold as cement, walking on rubber heels with stiff American gait as though to get somewhere someday and why not now just around the corner buy me a drink no then well so long and the hell with you.

Since I was here last everything has become younger, the whores included. The price is youth. Old whores are taken to the slaughterhouse and made into harnesses and straps and leather handles. Broadway is to the young, where the females are concerned. The males may be middle-aged, bald, fat, amorphous, cockeyed, lop-sided, bile-ridden, rheumy, asthmatic, arthritic – *but the women must be young!* They must be young and fresh and tough and durable, like the new buildings, the new elevators, the new cars, the stainless-steel knives and forks that never wear out and are just as sharp and efficacious as Gorham silver blades. Broadway is full of jowl-faced, lynx-eyed lawyers and politicians, all smartly dressed, white-starched collars, the correct tie, the latest patch pocket. Everybody has a crease in his trousers and shoes highly polished. Nobody wears a last year's hat, crisis or no crisis. Nobody is without a clean handkerchief softly laundered and wrapped in a seal packer-chief. When you have your hair brushed by the barber he throws the brush away to be fumigated and wrapped in cello-phane again. The cloth he puts around your neck is sent imme-diately to the laundry – by pneumatic air tubes that deliver the following morning. Everything is a twenty-four-hour service, whether it is necessary or not. Your things come back so fast you don't have time to earn the money to pay for this service you don't need. If it rains you get your shoes shined just the same – because the polish is a protection against weather stains. You get trimmed coming and going. You are in the sausage machine and there is no way out – unless you take a boat and go somewhere else. Even then you can't be sure because the whole fucking world is going a hundred percent American. It's a disease.

All this leads me back to the great American novel – *Of Time and the River*[18] – now being advertised in all the Fifth Avenue buses. This is one of those great American novels which is always heralded as *the* great American novel but which somehow is forgotten after a month or so because the props which made up the scaffolding are so rotten that they fall apart. Like all the other great American novels this one is space filler. *Time and the River* are lost in space. There are three dimen-sions, but the fourth is lacking. It is a *Comédie Humaine* with Hannibal, Missouri, as the vital center. It proliferates as cancer proliferates. It does not burn, belch, roar, sizzle, fume, steam, fire, smoke. It starts, as all the great American novels start, at the big toe – and works upward. In travelling up the tibia you get lost. You get lost in the follicles of that superfluous hair which the American women are always removing from their legs and arms. A really great book starts in the midriff and works outward. It starts vitally and ends vitally. It is vital through and through. The architecture comes about not through a desire to fill space but because hunger and faith demand an edifice, a testimony, a concrete symbol and resting place. Perhaps I am unfair to this great American author: I admit that I read only about forty pages. But in forty pages a man, or his soul – if he has one – must unlimber. True, there were emotional swells – but they were like bloated frescoes which one takes in out of the corner of his eye while running a marathon. Altogether too goddamned genealogical to suit my taste! I detest all books which run chronologically, which commence at the cradle and end with the grave. Even life doesn't run that way, much as people think it does. Life only commences at the hour of spiritual birth – which may be at eighteen or at forty-seven. And death is never the goal – but life! more life! Someone must throw a pitchfork into this river of space–time which the Americans have created; the rivers must be made to run uphill, against the grain. Like the St. Johns River! Here as fast as new rivers are created dikes are built to hem them in – to make them work, to make them pay. We need a flood, and only then will there be a rich silt to work with. We don't need genealogical novels, or the story of the American continent seen through the eyes of the Swiss Family Robinson. Somebody has got to throw a monkey wrench into the works. I feel that I'm the guy, Joey, to make the rivers run uphill. I owe it to the American buffalo and the red Indian, to the shades of Montezuma and the Quetzalcoatl. In order to accomplish this task I have already cut off my head. I am going to walk down the open street, Broadway preferably, with my head in hand and all the gas mains belching a sweet stench. I am going to walk along with my head in my hands and have a look at things astrologically. I already feel lighter, springier, gayer. Perhaps I will leave my head at the Villa Seurat and just walk with the rest of my body down Broadway. I will carry the book with me, a big iron book clasped to my belt. In it I will record strange things. I shall be the high priest of the great American novel running uphill for the first time since the dawn of creation – *and ship some fine Westphalian hams to Jerusalem, please!*

Just had a letter from that old gal Juliet who asks – 'Why didn't you look us up before? Why do you have to make your *permanent* home in Paris? Why do you have to sail on June the 14th? Why do you continue to be expatriated?' I feel like answering that letter here and now. So here goes, Joey...

Dear Juliet,

The reason I didn't look you up before this is because I forgotten about you completely. It was only the other night, when I was a little soused and had ordered an expensive cigar, that seeing the label on the cigar I remembered you were alive and had a kid. The reason I make my *permanent* home in Paris is because I am a millionaire and can afford to have a home wherever I please. The reason I sail June the 14th is because another day here would drive me nuts; had you written me a few days earlier I could have saved myself the trouble of writing this letter by sending you a copy of the preceding pages which explain everything. You say that things are so exciting in America that it is difficult for you to imagine establishing yourself elsewhere. That's all right for you to say since you are only a mother and the wife of the editor of a third-rate swindle sheet. You live on the socio-economic plane. I am living on the astronomic plane which you can reach only if you have a pair of wings. You say that you read my book 'not without interest,' which is a curious negative way of putting it – but what about your husband, the editor, to whom I sent a copy for review at my own expense? Why hasn't that bastard given me a review? A stick at least? Isn't there enough sociology in it for his swindle sheet? My next book will be about the functional work habits of the cockroach during the Civil War – which I think will be up his street. It will describe the endocrine system with and without food, showing the relation between climatic changes and periods of unemployment. It will have a dull cover, such as the government tracts are bound in, and small type, and an errata at the back. It is too bad I never read any of your husband's verse. All my knowledge of him comes from Joe Gould. Joe Gould said he would piss on him one day and make a man of him. Is that true? Anyway, that's what they tell me. And now let me tell you something about the baby – about bringing it up properly. When you feed him his oats always pour a little lukewarm horse piss into the mush. This will put backbone into him and later, when he becomes an editor, he will not need to be pissed on by a neglected American author in order to become a man. If you want him to become an erudite read him Kenneth Burke's translation of *The City Man* – it makes a fine slumber song. And why do you insist on washing the baby's diapers? Use Kotex. It costs no more, and it's sanitary. Order a box today from the Smithsonian Institute. 'By exercising care, courtesy and common sense,' as Police Commissioner Valentine counsels, 'you and yours may live long and happily.' Please remember that. So long, Juliet... you were always a good cigar... but rather expensive. Signed: Henry Valentine Miller.

Did you like that, Joey? Maybe you can think up some more cunts we can write to. They don't need to write me. Just forward their names and addresses. This is the open season for letters. If I had money I wouldn't write another line. I would go to a bar and order a sandwich and a glass of beer. I would look up Stefano Fanti who calls me by name whenever I visit his joint. He makes me feel good. He says: 'I let you buy all the drinks you want; when you get ready to leave *I buy you a drink*.' He says that to our face. No cunning in that. Right out with it. That's what I like about Europeans. They don't give you something for nothing. You must pay and pay through the nose. Here everything is free, cheap as a song, but it costs more than you can afford. It seems wonderful at first not to leave a tip when you go to a bar or a drugstore. No tips! Sounds like Utopia. But when you count your change you find that you paid three times as much for a drink as you would in Europe, *pourboire compris*. I figure I've paid these soda water jerkers royal tips all along. They've been fucking me – maybe not the jerkers themselves, but the proprietors then, i.e., The Great Atlantic & Pacific Tea Co.

It just occurs to me that it's a pity I was not sent over by the *Paris-Soir*, along with Blaise Cendrars and Claude Farrère.[19] I would have earned my passage back by this time, to say nothing of the free champagne and the Corona-Coronas. Perhaps my style is not good enough for the *Paris-Soir* – but then, is Claude Farrère's? Can you imagine what that bird's going to say about the *Normandie?* And how does Cendrars manage to hold himself down? Does he dictate his copy? You see, I have all the equipment, including carbon paper. I would be the most inexpensive reporter they could possibly find. If they didn't like that letter I just wrote to Juliet they could cut it out. I remember how, in the early days, I used to buy *Le Journal* for breakfast – that was my morning exercise. I remember those cheesy articles dispatched by Maurice Dekobra – here and there an English phrase (misspelled) to lend a little local color. I remember the guy they sent to India, the guy who wrote so charmingly about the *pavillion des fleurs*. I remember the bike races reported by Paul Morand – or if not Morand then some other pretentious nitwit. All these things could do with my left hand – *and at less than the cost of ordinary ground burial*. Of course, I would have to do them in English. That's it – I am condemned to write in English to a people who do not exist. I might just as well begin to study Chinese. I am sure the Chinese would be more appreciative. (Free ad: Read *The Hanging on Union Square!* Written in English by one, Tchiang, a Chinaman. *Ta, ta, ta, ta! Money gone, nobody home. Ta, ta, ta, ta!* That's from the poems. The novel is in colloquial pidgin English, fresh from Union Square and the Rand School of Social Sciences.) Mr Tchiang is one of my favorite authors. I have forgotten who the others are. Ezra Pound probably. Someday I am going to read Ezra Pound. I am going to read the *Unfinished Cantos* at a gallop. And then I am going to read Gertrude Stein and Unamuno.[20] If I have more time I shall get down to reading the *Fourth Eclogue* – and perhaps the three preceding *Eclogues*. And now I am going to call a brief halt and take a nap. It is four o'clock Eastern Standard Time; if I sleep fast I can wake up at exactly the same time in Nagasaki or Mozambique. I do hate to lose time, time being the only precious thing I possess. So I will snooze a while to restore my waning powers in order to go on with this letter which I am sure must be of great interest to you and the readers of *Paris-Soir*. Don't forget to remind me of the man I saw shining his own shoes. He was a bootblack and business was so bad that he had to shine his own shoes. I can't get over it. Times are really bad, I guess.

Passing the Woolworth Building today on the elevated line I couldn't help but notice how like a Nuremberg cheese cake this piece of architecture now seems. This is the skyscraper that only a few years ago they were praising the shit out of because of its modernity. Designed by one of the best American architects. And today it looks cheesy. Not only cheesy, but insignificant. It looks like an angel cake with birthday candles on it. The same for the Metropolitan Tower and the Singer Building. They look woebegone. They belong to the past, that past which has no place in America, which crumbles at a breath. I notice that the great cathedrals never seem outmoded. The pedant may see in them this century or that; but a man like myself who walks the streets aimlessly is completely indifferent to the centuries represented. For him they are timeless. They will inspire a hundred years from now, five hundred years from now, a thousand years from now – if the Germans haven't destroyed them. The feeling I have about America, about the whole continent – flora, fauna, architecture, peoples, customs – is this: *nothing vital was ever begun here… nothing of value.* As far as I can determine, nothing ever will get started, in this deep, vital sense. They can blow things up to the most colossal proportions, make a network of cities which will obliterate the now intervening countryside – still it will make no difference. It is a horizontal movement – *space-filling* – and consequently futile. Tomorrow the whole continent might sink into the sea – and what would be lost? Is there one priceless monument? One irreplaceable thing? Anything whose loss would create a feeling of real deprivation, such as the loss of Dante's great work, for example?

And now, Joey, I'm going to get serious for a moment. I'm going to say a few words about the aeroplane, about that obsession for the air which seems to have the Americans by the balls. I want to ask you what it means, this business of flying to the moon, or Mars, or Jupiter? I ask myself very seriously if this flying mania is not the symptom of a very great and very real distress, if it does not mean something more than just a conquest of the air, as they say. It's all right to say that the aviator is connecting one city with another, that he's cutting down the time element, establishing new modes of communication, etc. But that's not all – that's not the whole story. There is another and deeper element which enters into it, and that's the awakening of a mystic sense. The aviator rises above the earth and revolves with the earth, or almost. He moves with the stars in a new dimension, or he has the illusion of so doing. He feels a sense of power, not as of old – in touching the earth – but in freeing himself from the earth. This is dangerous. In another hundred years he will be thinking astrologically again. He will have developed the flying sense, he will be drunk with the feel of the cosmos, with new space–time ideas, just as Europe was drunk with the discovery of America. He will say to himself that it is his ambition to reach the moon, or Mars, or Jupiter, but he will never reach the moon – he will reach to himself again, to man, to a new fury of creative activity. Each time a new horizon is opened up, each time the imaginative horizon is enlarged, the earth becomes smaller and more habitable. Life does not spread: it blooms, it burgeons, it develops in intensity. Now men think it is important to get from one place to another more quickly. Tomorrow they will stand stock-still, content to go nowhere. They will stand stock-still and sing about travelling to incalculable realms. There is only one road for man, and that is towards God. Along this road, if he searches and prays, he meets himself. Then he opens wide his jaws and sings with all his might. Then he doesn't need God anymore – God then is everywhere distant as the farthest planet, close as his own skin. We are going towards God, I say, in the aeroplane. No aeroplane will ever reach God. No *man* will ever reach God. But we can have Hallelujah, and when a man has found himself it is Hallelujah all the time. I have found it without hiring an aeroplane. I found it standing in a pair of moccasins.

And now, brother Fredl, I want you to make ready a little song. Up, up, up in my flying machine! We are going to sing this standing on the higher ground. We will stand on the last stanza of *Faust* and get that ever-higher feeling. Towards the eternal feminine, which, after all, is only the drag and pull of Nature, which, when one becomes altogether Godlike, says: Be yourself! Touch the earth! Let us, therefore, rise in song and fall with the parachute. Goethe, standing on that last stanza, commanded a greater vista than any aviator has yet commanded. He was standing on the higher middle ground, the metaphysical table-land which is between heaven and earth. Poised on the eternal moment, calm, sure, prince of men, he surveyed past and future. He saw the spiral motion which obtains in all realms, commencing with the astral and finishing with the astral. He saw it in its unendingness. Goethe was an aviator a hundred years before his time. He learned to stand still – *and sing*.

And now, Joey, before hopping the boat I want to give you a little more precise information about the Empire State Building – a few facts and figures which will make your hair stand on end. It's like this... beyond the 13th story no more vertigo, because the speed of ducks flying towards the Equator is in inverse ratio to the sound of shot falling through space at 865,000,947 miles a second. The windows are rainproof, the walls fireproof. Lingerie and toilet articles on the 227th floor. Since this building was erected there have been 765,492,583 visitors to the mooring mast, all of them equipped with parachutes and false teeth. This is the tallest building in the world 'irregardless of' the flagpole where throughout 365 days and nights Old Glory flies 'irregardless of' snow, rain, sleet, hail, mist, fog, bank panics or no bank panics. The janitors, who comprise a force slightly larger than the standing armies of Europe, are equipped with holeproof socks and bulletproof jockstraps.

They have been tested for intelligence and are extremely courteous even when underpaid. The entire staff, with the exception
of the night force, is fumigated each evening in order to avoid
the outbreak of epidemics such as typhoid, yellow fever, dysentery and similar contagious diseases. This is the most wonderful
building in the world with the exception of those still more
wonderful buildings now in course of construction which will
outdo everything past and present including the ones to come
concerning which we can give as yet no precise figures as all the
returns are not in yet. However, it looks like a landslide.

The most marvellous thing about this most marvellously
marvellous building is the gift shop on the 267th floor where
you change elevators to fly to the 318th floor situated at the
base of the mooring mast which rises from here to the dizzy
height of 563 stories. Here you may find every bauble and
trinket known to civilized man, not least of which is a mena-
gerie of figurines made entirely of chewing gum – *Wrigley's*
chewing gum. The man whose inventive genius made possible
this assemblage of chewing gum figurines was a *chiclero* from
the jungle of Yucatan. After a long and honorable career he was
discharged by the chewing gum magnates without notice. Said
genius may be interviewed any day at the Barbizon-Plaza where
courtesy dwells. Here, free of the chewing gum barons, he now
makes his abode. Other remarkable gifts are picture postcards
showing front, back and side views of every building in New
York 'irregardless of' size or content. Also views from the roof –
and stereopticon slides. A word of caution to the casual visitor:
do not handle the objects!

Despite its prodigious dimensions this giant skyscraper was
erected in less than six months, thanks to the splendid aeroplane
interfactories service through the co-operation of the Carpenters
& Joiners Guild. It may interest you to know that by the terms
of the contract the building called for completion at noon, the

12th of February. Due, however, to the splendid co-operation aforementioned, the building was entirely erect and all the windows washed at nine o'clock the morning of February 12th. The contract did not call for the windows to be washed: this was a gratuitous contribution of the Window Cleaners Union. We wish to dispel here and now any false rumors that may have been circulated by hostile unions as to the quality of light emitted through these windows. The light is absolutely pure and filtered, and the tower management guarantees faultless vision of not less than 75 miles under normal barometrical conditions. Such a guarantee could only be offered the public thanks to the latest installation of thermostats manufactured expressly for *Empire State*. In addition to faultless vision the thermostats also insure an even pressure on the eardrums when dropping from the top of the mooring mast to the subbasement which, it has been estimated, is approximately a half-mile below sea level. This is a device absolutely unique in the history of skyscrapers and will prove a boon to all those who suffer from phthisis and dyspnoeia, the latter sometimes referred is internal catarrh.

The casual observer may have been impressed by a phenomenal sight whilst eating a steak sandwich at the base of the tower. The canaries which warble so melodiously in their platinum cages are not here to entertain the visitor while lunching, as one might imagine, but to overcome an inclination to fall asleep when gazing out the windows. These canaries, unlike their fellow canaries, do not warble to pass the time away. On the contrary, they warble to restore the sense of time which is endangered whenever the human organism is subjected to the unreality of altitudes to which his pedestrian habits make him maladapted. The canaries have been skilfully trained by a staff of expert endocrinologists working in conjunction with the best psychoanalysts of New York State. They warble just loud enough to cross the subliminal threshold of the acoustic nerve centers, thus lulling the transient visitor back to a triphammer rhythm of daily life whence he may look out upon a familiar world without fear of agoraphobia, hydrophobia, or any perverse or polymorphous disturbances. The canaries are released every night at nine o'clock sharp in order to be examined by diplomaed throat specialists. This amazing service is due in part to the memory of Gatti-Cazzazza who, in anticipation of this great need, ordered his confidential attorney to add a codicil to his last will and testament. The visitor will observe that on the underside of every cage the head of this great benefactor has been embossed in solid gold.

In anticipating the eventual decline of New York City as a financial and industrial center the owners of *Empire State*, heretofore known as Empire State Corporation, Inc., cede to the State of New York all vested rights and preoccupations with its skyscraper modus operandi. No cost will be spared by said management to keep the unemployed workers of this great and glorious State in a permanent condition of content. The halls on the ground floor, deliberately given a sombre cast in deference to the national crisis, will be redecorated in bright colors, with frescoes especially designed by artists of international repute to prevent melancholy or morbidity. These frescoes will depict the gay and turbulent life of New York when the factories were working overtime and sirloin steaks were selling at $5.79 a pound. Profiting by the experience of Greece and Babylon, of Egypt and China, New York State intends to keep its monuments in a fit state of preservation, applying with great therapeutic insight and benevolence the pragmatic wisdom of her great pioneers and inventors, the Ghouls and the Breakwaters.

This gigantic structure, replete in all its parts, will be in its old age the refuge of the poor and needy, a haven for the industrious paupers whose sweat and toil, or *without* whose sweat and toil, these things could not, *sui generis*, have been made *de facto* and *ad hoc.* It has been estimated that with the depopulation of the city and the loss of the migratory worker no more healthful site than the Empire State could found in these precincts. The ugly buildings of preskyscraper age will be razed in order to afford an unobstructed view of the Statute of Liberty. Said statute will be scraped and varnished and, from the neck up, studded with precious stones which will gleam in the night, thus eliminating the cost of electric wiring. Positively no expense will be spared to make *Empire State* an enduring monument to progress and invention...

Aboard the Veendam, 3rd or 4th day out.
Here I am on the horary ocean, reading Doc Williams' *A Novelette and Other Prose.*[21] This calls for a special letter to Doc Williams... *Also:*

Dear Doc Williams:
We are now in midocean and it is snowing, or should be, if it were just a little colder. Cape Race is a little to the left and north. We are going right and north. The back end of the boat is for the ventilators – and the steerage passengers. This makes the trip even more enjoyable than one would otherwise imagine, the sour bilge rising gently out of the funnels and billowing through all the portholes to starboard and fore and aft. At noon a slick young man from Amherst says: 'Now folks, I want you all to listen to this... this is very serious: if you have not yet signed up for the ping-pong tournament please do so tonight.' He says he will announce to us from time to time just what is happening, or going to happen, or not yet happened. Without him the boat would not run properly. We would be bored. We would all commit suicide and so, when we arrived at port, there would be no passengers disembarking. You can see how important, *and serious*, this is. I am thinking of moving up to first class and dining with the captain.

Dear Doc Williams, this is about your *Novelette and Other Prose* which I am enjoying. About *Tender Buttons*²² and the obscenity of James Joyce. While reading you I also was reading Keyserling – Count Hermann²³ of *America Set Free*. This is a very tender button of a book also. Count Hermann is a philosopher – I want you to get that straight. He is a philosopher by virtue of the fact that he is constantly philosophizing. There is another book which I am reading between the two – my own. I see that we are all saying the same thing: that America is a dunghill.

The Count, he sees the roses growing already. *You* see only the asphalt roads! I don't see anything – not very far anyhow. Just now, please remember, I am in midocean. The ocean gets into your consciousness. It is impossible to dislodge it. There is too much of it, and not enough of sky and water. That is why sailors are usually cracked. Cracked before and after. Cracked all the time. From too much ocean. *Voila!* I thought I was going to begin another book aboard the boat. But I didn't reckon with the ocean. The man who can write a book on board a boat must be even more lonely than the ocean itself. He must be bigger than the ocean.

What struck me particularly in your *Novelette* was the reference to Van Gogh. 'Van Gogh, realizing the light, fought blindly to paint it and to live it. But died, naturally. One cannot eat sand – and the world would not give itself to be eaten.' I used almost the same language in writing about Lawrence. This business of eat and be eaten – I don't think it is understood at all today... However, what impresses me about your work is that the fragments are so much greater than the whole. In your prose you write whole poems. The poems seem fragmented. But what you convey effectively is the clean, white striving, the takeoff, the eye focussing calmly, not knowing, but venturing, each stride a new dimension, always a new world beyond, *and always danger with entire success.* You seem to have realized the nature of the skeleton, the structural harmony of an antithetical world. You talk about the meat all the time, the white fringe of the world not thoroughly digested, making one belch, causing somnolence and flatulence. I don't know where you talk this exactly, but it is there. You say things diametrically the wrong way, which I understand perfectly, because each time you start from scratch and bury into significance. Your lines come to a dead halt against the bone, like a bullet crashing through the brain, flattening against the occipital bone. The words burn through, splatter – a dull thud and then rest. There is no weariness, as in watching skyrockets. No ennui, as at Versailles, the fountains playing, the pigeons cooing. You seem to have grasped the meaning of tradition, through the study of compound fractures. You set the enzymes free, leaving a clear field for decomposition.

End of letter to Doc Williams

The thing about an ocean voyage is that travelling Dutch you sometimes have a lunatic aboard. A crazy Dutchman is more of a lunatic than an ordinary lunatic. We have on board a Dutchman who was so out of work that he walked up to the Consul one day and gave him a pair of black eyes. He is making the voyage in the brig. Every hour or so he sends the captain a message – 'My meal was not delivered on time this morning... I would like to have a cigar... ' Etc., etc. He looks through his little porthole, which is barred, and reports on the weather. He smokes good cigars, at government expense. He is smiling all the time, partly because he is Dutch and good-natured, partly because he is crazy. Those who are not crazy aboard the boat also smile a great deal – that is, those who are Dutch. The Dutch have nothing to do but smile. The dikes are all completed, you see, and the tulips planted. Ergo, smile! When you sit down to breakfast the first thing you do is to make yourself a cheese sandwich, with caraway seeds. *This settles your stomach!* The Dutch caraway seed, I must add in passing, is slightly lacking in alcoholic content. It is reddish in color and easily digested. If dropped in a glass of Heineken beer it turns acid. This brings about a belching which releases the poison gases heretofore locked up in the cloaca maxima. The urinals are all equipped with brass rails which must be polished before 10.00 a.m. when the captain makes his usual inspection. After that it is time to peel the potatoes. Also at 10.00 a.m. each morning the band begins to play. A three-piece orchestra with piano accompaniment. The music is Dutch: no sky and water. Oceanic music, complete from beginning to end. And slightly lenitive. The first piece is usually 'Immer Oder Nimmer.' This gives the morning the proper spiritual cast. You remember, first a cheese sandwich, then the brass rails, then the potatoes, then – 'Oder Nimmer Oder Schwimmer.'[24] Followed by 'The Blue Danube Waltz.' The Dutch are international in taste – that is, *strictly neutral*. They smile a great deal...

A gruesome fact about the voyage thus far is the preponderance of books. It is like a colony of ants coming aboard, each one equipped with enough provender to last out the longest voyage. In case you haven't brought a book with you Miss Pfeiffer, the librarian of the Holland–America Line, will rent you a book from the ocean lending library. There is a plethora of books. Everybody reads – even the nut in the brig. Nobody says anything. People seem to be afraid to be left alone with one another. There are a few intelligent-looking individuals on board with whom I should like to talk, but they are shy. When you see someone coming towards you you smile politely and say 'How do you do!' – which is to prevent further intimacy. This 'how do you do' business goes on all day long, each time you pass someone – twenty, thirty, forty times a day. Being polite and courteous is a way of holding your neighbor at arm's length. It freezes him out. Checkmate! Or, stalemate!

Another thing… when I get up in the morning I always forget that I am on the Veendam. I seem to think that I am travelling on the Champlain: I seem to remember better those faces of six months ago than these new ones which I see every day. I remember the old faces because they were such jolly faces. They were French, for the most part. They laughed and danced and played pranks on one another all during the trip. There were no flowers on the table – but plenty of wine. Here the cheapest wine you can get costs fifty cents a split, which is a pint in American. The Dutch people do not drink with their meals. They have a glass of beer *after* the meal, so it was explained to me.

And now, Joey, I will tell you a little more about the American faces which I see on board, why America will soon become like the Netherlands and every boat have flowers and a cow with big fat udders that gives plenty of creamy milk. The American face is best studied by examining the young people who are touring Europe this summer. Most of the young fellows wear their hair close-cropped, like the Germans. They have all been fumigated first, please remember. The idea is to lie in the sun as much as possible and get that outdoor complexion. You must also remember to wear tweeds and rubber-soled shoes; if possible, carry a pipe. The lips should be thin, the eyes bleak, the face well set, like Portland cement. Now and then there should be a thin smile, from one corner of the mouth to the other – no further. A *painful* smile, if possible. One should always look as if he were thinking of extremely complicated matters – the destiny of mankind, the price of wheat, the new ocean freight rates. One should have a pad on his knee and between profound glances at the sea look up sternly, quizzically, and twiddle his thumbs. If someone approaches with apparent intent to talk, and if one does not mean to be frozenly polite, then one should suddenly jump to his feet, push the right hand forward briskly, and say: 'My name is So-and-so... *and yours please?*' This is certain to make things click. If one were to start in without this hand-jerking, trigger-pulling introduction things might go wrong. One might say the wrong thing to the wrong person. This would produce ultimate chaos...

The reason why it is so wonderfully difficult to write books for America is because America is an ocean. There is so much of and to America that one cannot see the sky or the water. Only the ocean. One is adrift on an endless body of water for ten or twelve days. People come and go. Your life is mapped out for you by the company, and it seems very regular, very well regu-lated. Actually you feel chaotic. You feel that you are running with the herd and the herd is on the stampede. Nobody knows where he is going, but he keeps close to his neighbor – he feels safer that way, more at ease. If suddenly someone were to stand still, not follow the herd, a catastrophe would ensue. To prevent this there is a band on board. At the first sign of panic the music starts up. Then everybody commences to revolve around his neighbor again and you have that delightful *confiture* called Dutch Jam which you will find on the menu, second line from the bottom between Bread-and-Butter. There is no extra charge for the bread and butter. It is free, like the music. Like the ocean, which you can't get out of your consciousness.

We are now entering the northern circle – to prove that the shortest distance between two points is a curved line. The air is chilly, the water full of white caps. A trade wind is blowing down from the Arctic Ocean.

Interruption while the musikers play 'The Kaiser Parade' in *dreivierteltakt*.[25] The band has just finished with 'The Polar Star,' a mazurka. Between renditions the violinist clucks like a hen. He is laying the eggs for his next voyage. At four o'clock some Harvard lads will come down from the Tourist class to give us some jazz. I prefer to listen to the Dutch three-piece string orchestra: it is full of sheep and meadow lands, of babbling brooks and tables set with ham and jam. All this stinks a little bit, but it is a better stink than the drone and trickle of the jazz band. After all, the Dutch orchestra is surrealistic. It is full of little surprises – 'Put in an Old Pair of Shoes,' for instance. Whenever things lag the orchestra strikes up a Wienerschnitzel Waltz. This waltz is composed of the dead flowers from yesterday's table, plus a few caraway seeds, some flat Holland cheese and the 'cellist's false teeth which, by the way, are strung on wires just like a puppet show. Whenever the 'cellist wishes to smile he smiles first with his teeth. He warns you just a moment in advance. Gradually the whole mouth opens, showing the coated tongue, the tonsils, the palate and the insulation. The jazz band, on the other hand, is composed strictly of undergraduates: they know nothing about caraway seeds, babbling sheep, dead flowers, false teeth, etc. The drummer plays with wire brooms: they look like ordinary brooms which have been plucked. The music requires no direction; it comes out like toothpaste. Not even notes are required. Just a toothbrush and a wire broom.

Today, as I said before, it is a very chill day. Today of all days the captain chooses to have the sailors clean the rigging. There they are, up in the rigging, with pails and sponges. The captain's orders. Meanwhile the captain sits on the poop deck, which is first class, with the society dames, looking through his opera glasses. He has warm white gloves on. And the sailors, poor buggers, the sailors are dancing the hornpipe with cold. Their hands look like boiled steaks. Meanwhile the boat is getting whiter and whiter. Why? What for? To make an impression? On whom? For me the boat was already white enough. Why the hell must it be whiter? Maybe they are expecting the albatross!

Maybe it's all part of the stern discipline which makes he-men of the sailors. Probably keeps them from buggering one another in the hold. But it's all very sad and futile. The real trouble is – there is not enough work to go around! When there is not enough *real* work one must clean and scrub, make things white, or whiter. This is the foul, lying basis on which honesty and sobriety are reared. Make the boat white! Tomorrow, or the next day, it will be dirty again. Well, boat no clean, boat no sail good. Oceanic logic!

One of the interesting nuts on board the boat is the Armenian opera singer who shares my cabin. Every day he asks, in French, 'What day is it today?' If I say 'Thursday' he answers: 'Good! Then tomorrow is Sunday!' Every day he asks, in French, how many more days before we arrive? If you say five days he says, 'Good, then we will be there tomorrow!' Alone with himself he packs and unpacks his valises. He transfers the contents of one grip to another. Then he locks and unlocks, trying out all his keys. Then he gets ready to shave. He is always just about to shave. As he is an Armenian, you see, his beard grows very fast. To everybody he says: '*Vous parlez français, Madame, ou Monsieur?*'[26] He even asks the Dutch sailors – '*Vous parlez français, Monsieur?*' The point is, he wants to make sure. The joke is, he hardly knows any French himself. But he likes to hear the language spoken. And so the whole boat, third class at least, is now speaking French. Everybody has learned to say – '*Vous parlez français, Monsieur, ou Madame?*' Anyhow, *vass goot*, as the Hollanders say.[27] This morning Maatjes herring for breakfast. Noon meatballs. No wine. No champagne. No cordials. Only Heineken beer, very light and frothy. Like whipped cream turning sour.

Anyway, the masts have all been washed, the spittoons rinsed, the brown tablecloths set. Tonight we will see Lillian Harvey in 'Let's Live Tonight!' I wish it were a pornographic film *sans suite* instead. '*Vous parlez français, Monsieur?*'

Thursday, aboard the Veendam.

Conversation the whole morning long with Herr Speck of Rotterdam, also third class. Conversation reminds me of the difficulty of communicating with the world. Herr Speck came from Rotterdam twelve years ago and found a job with the Fisher Body Company where he is now a foreman or something. He wants every day that he should learn something new so that he can understand what is the world. Sometimes when he sits by himself and thinks he almost goes crazy; he has to stop thinking and play cards, or talk with his wife who is more American in her ways, i.e., *more romantisch*. We were standing at the taffrail looking down at the water. Herr Speck said he had been studying the color of the water, why it was so green sometimes, and finally this morning he had come to the conclusion that it must be the dirty dishwater and the garbage they dump overboard now and then. He said that made the water greasy and hence it got green-looking, like when you was sick and that dirty stuff come up from your stomach like. I said – you mean *bile*. He said – Yah, I call it billyus in Holland. He said every day he was in the same mood, always quiet like und content; he couldn't understand why it was that some days men look happy and the next day they are melancholy. When I go to bed, he says, I yoost drop all my thoughts, yoost like my clothes. My wife she say I have only one leg in the bed and I be asleep already. Herr Speck says he is always restless and active, unless he is thinking. When I wake up I yump right out of bed... I want to see what iss going on in de voorld... I can't lay in bed... I am too nervous for dot. He says it is wonderful how broad-minded the Americans are – not like Hollander vot never leaves his little village. Dot iss because the Americans they have the sense to eddicate the people right away in the English language. Not like Belgium, which is a backvord country all the time because the Wals have only 4,500,000 people and they want that the

Flandres should speak French too. Over hundert yahrs go vass Belgiums separated yon Holland peoples. Dot vass very bad for Belgiums people. United States iss much better peoples. Everybody vork und get ahead. Only ting foolish iss de money – money make people foolish so they get lazy und tink nothing but pleasure all de time. No developpement de mind so dot everybody be eddicated and become success what you call it in life.

Herr Speck likes to read *deep* books – not dot romantischer trash vot his wife so foolishly reads. He like vot you call de 'Digest.' Vass goot, de 'Digest,' cause everything is quick und no foolishnesses. He likes vot you call *deep* books – und not *luff* all the time. I am a man always alone, says Herr Speck. Sometime I listen for a while und den ven I vass polite I take a back seat vot you say und I sit down und I tink. I vood like more to be as American peoples vot are happy und gay, vot talk about dere motor cars, how fast dey go und such tings, but I vass very lonely all de time und I must feerst understand vot it all iss by myself. Dot iss my happiness – ven I can sit down and understand vot iss de voorld. I never laugh at people, even ven dey ask me foolish questions. I tink always dot dot man vot I talk to he haf someting sensible to ask only he don't know vell how to say it. Everybody hass brain und vant to know someting about de voorld. Vee must eddicate de peoples to ask questions, odervise vee vill nenfer learn sometings. You haf read, I suppose, dot book by Van Loon – vere he talks aboud man vot he come from de chipanazis vot you call it. I tink myself sometime dot fellow Van Loon he iss too fantastisch. He go too far mit de chipanazis. Man he iss someting spirchel vot I say, all de time. Odervise he vood be yoost an animal, iss it not? Van Loon he say onct dot man haf big mooscles like all ape und a tiny little brain vot makes hiss head too small for de body. Vass long time ago, he say – maybe 3,000 yahr ago, ven it vass vot you call de flood. I don't know if dot iss right voord for it – my eddication in de

57

English iss not so goot anymore. I vass only four months be de night school... I vork hard all day. Anyway, he say dere vass big animals vot now iss only de bones in de eerd. I tink dot iss foolish say 3,000 yahr ago dere vass animals like dot vot nobody ever saw. Dot iss vot I call fantastischer writing. I don't like ven he talk dot way aboud de eerd. Dot makes like I vass foolish und he smarter vot I am. Odervise he is writing very goot books, very sensible and dick und deep. Like sometime I go listen to opera vonce awhile. Vass goot musik und beautiful. I like vot iss beautiful also vonce awhile. A man must eddicate himself so he can enjoy de musik von de opera. My wife she say everybody iss tired ven I talk such tings. She like to play cards all night und read dot trash vot iss de magazines. She becomes qvicker vot I do an American... maybe because she iss a vooman und vooman must half always light tings...

Here we talk for a space about the foramenifera, the different strata of earth and what they are composed of, all in accordance with Herr Speck's reading of the *Literary Digest*. He tells me I should go ahead and explain him what was the world before the flood because that is what he knows the least about. He thanks me in advance because he knows that when I get through he will know a little more than when he started, and that will make him feel better for the rest of the day. And so, after a while, we come back to man's spiritual nature in which Herr Speck is vitally interested – because he does not want to be yoost an animal vot can't tink. He says everything would turn out well if only we all loved one another. I don't call dot luff, says Herr Speck, ven two people get together und make each oder sick mit dere fever. Dot iss only de *fisical* vot I call it. Dot iss no better vass de animals, no? Here I venture to contradict Herr Speck. I try to explain to him that physical love is very important, perhaps more important than brotherly love. Herr Speck says he will now disagree with me – but now I will explain you vy.

Vot iss luff? It iss nodding. How long does it last? Two weeks? Vot iss dot? I call luff vot iss de *spirchel*, dot vot make man to understand de voorld. Luff iss not a dog in the street vot runs around de whole day mit his nose in de air. Is it so or not? Ven two people dey luff each oder, dot iss not luff. Dot iss de fisical. Dot iss ven de body talks. Und de body dot iss for de animals vot haf no sense und can not enjoy de ocean or de opera…

And so, by degrees, we come to President Roosevelt who is a great man in Herr Speck's opinion. President Roosevelt he say ven he vass elected: 'I cannot make a hit every time I come to the bat!' Dot vass a fine remark von President Roosevelt. Ya, he iss very big man, like his brother Teddy. I suppose you heerd von him, vot he vass doing in the Philippine Islands long ago? He vass great tinker also. Dot iss vy I say America makes good citizens…

(Interruption: the dinner bell is ringing!)

Friday, aboard the Veendam.
A few more pages, Joey, and I will be breaking my own record! This morning I copied out a little notice from the Mannen Toilet. It reads as follows:

> *Men wordt verzocht in de privaten niets te werpen, waardoor deze kunnen verstoppen, of het doorstrommen van water kan worden belemmerd.*[28]

Of course this is official Hollandisch. For real emotion I give you now Nana's last words, in Dutch:

> *'Ik zou je nooit iemand gelukkig gemaakt… Ook mezelf niet… zoo ben ik geboren.'*[29]

We do not return to dust, as the Bible says, but to the proto-plasmic slime which covers the floor of the ocean. Also – I just learned this today – the distance to the horizon line, standing on the poop deck, is only twelve miles. The reason one can't see further, the question of nearsightedness aside, is because the curvature of the earth drops one foot every five miles. This brings the bowsprit on a level with the keel of the ship just ahead. In nautical language this is called the 'geodesy' of the earth. It sounds all wet to me.

Last night we stayed up till midnight playing Kino. It's a game of *achtendacheter*, or *sesensester*.[30] The game took place in the third-class dining room and was enlivened by the presence of a few Luxembourgeoises, some Lithuanians, a few Czechs and Frieslanders, and one Zeelander. The latter grows roses in Ukiah, California. Black roses. He says it is important to watch the roots, or they get cancerous. Kino is played with Lotto cards and little hard berries which you place on the number when it is called. To play the game properly the Steward must tie a white bag around his waist; in the white bag are little round disks numbered from 1 to 90. *Achtenachtig* is the best number. The next best number is *sesensester*. It is well to have a glass of beer at your side so as not to fall asleep between the numbers. In the morning you must take a physic because the pudding never changes. Every day comes the Nesselrode pudding in a new guise. It tastes like the scrapings from the ventilators. As do the *pommes rissolées*. About ten-thirty there are cold meat sandwiches buttered and sprinkled with caraway seeds. If you want a shower you write your name on the sheet hanging up in the toilet. You must notify the toilet attendant in advance – about twenty minutes or so. This is so that he can turn on the steam for the hot water and open the closet door where the saltwater soap is kept.

The chief steward is a Haarlem man. It is he who directs the game of Kino. The first thing he does, as I explained a moment ago, is to tie the white bag around his waist. Then he sits down carefully and, as he pulls the little disk from the bag, he calls the number off – first in Dutch, then in English, then in German, then in French, then in Italian. As soon as someone yells Kino he calls the deck steward to his side, points genially to the winner, and then with a modest little flourish directs the deck steward to slowly read off the winning line, slowly, one number at a time. As the deck steward calls the number the chief steward, who is sitting comfortably beside him in his chair, with the white bag around his waist, slowly and painfully searches for the Lotto; when he has found the Lotto corresponding to the numbered disk he holds up his right hand and, after a due pause, repeats the number which the deck steward has just read off. I say 'just read off.' Actually an infinite time has elapsed between these two operations. But we are on the horary ocean and time here is just chicken feed. Anyway, after the deck steward has said Yah, all right! the Chief Steward says OK go ahead, and so the next winning number on the winning line of the winning card is read off. If during this phase of the game the deck steward should happen to be called on deck the chief steward calls a temporary halt during which everybody sits calmly and smiles. To delegate the task of reading off the winning line to somebody else, to the toilet room attendant say, would be unthinkable. This is the deck steward's job and no mistake about it. You see, when you take a Dutch boat it may not be so fast, and it may not be so gay, but it is clean and safe and there are no mistakes. If you happen to speak Luxembourg dialect – what is called the *Gukkuk* you remember – then there are even less chances of making a mistake. All these languages derive from Low German and that is why the Wals, though they are only 4,500,000, will not have it to be interfered with by the Flems who do not know how to speak French anyway. That is why the Frieslanders, for example, say – '*Vest mit bestreepte pantalon en dessin moderne.*'[31] The basis of Dutch is a crazy quilt of dark brown colors for the most part. That is why they are filling in the Zuider Zee – because it does not pay to have skating just in the winter. The sugar, by the way, is made of cane and very coarse. The milk is not skimmed. The potatoes are greasy. The meat is always soup meat. The pudding is Nesselrode. The beer is Heineken beer and does not give you a headache. The beer is taken *after* meals. The spittoons are rinsed twice a day, oftener if necessary.

You mustn't get the impression, by the way, that the Dutch are lacking in intelligence. On the contrary, I should say they are very intelligent, even more so than the seal or the otter. For example, putting a salted herring on the salad! The first six days, you must understand, we had nothing but plain lettuce leaves, undressed. However, when the cook observed that nobody was eating the salad anymore he promptly (i.e., six days later – prompt for the Dutch!) brought out the salted herrings and had them laid across the lettuce leaves. The result is that one eats the lettuce leaves in order to get the taste of herring out of his mouth. These herrings, I must also remark, are not the ordinary Maatjes variety, such as abound in the North Sea. No, this is a long, snake-like herring with a rather flat head; the eyes are dull and glassy and the gills rather bloody-looking. The skin of this herring is black and rather difficult to rip off, but then this is compensated for by the fact that the herring is no longer greasy and slippery. You can hold the herring firmly with one hand and bite the head off at a gulp. If the lettuce leaves are still a little wet this gives the herring just the right flavor. Because the herring, like every other form of life, is basically 'protoplasmic.' Or, as Maasenduyckvansten, the great Dutch poet, put it: '*Van op het doorstroopen uit iemand belemmerd.*' Roughly translated, this means – 'Whoever bites gently knows great peace in his soul.'[32]

The Dutch tongue coming to me rather naturally, owing to my low parentage, I am now going on to a study of the prevailing dialects. In my next instalment I shall probably have a few words to say about the Wriessischer tongue. The peculiar characteristic of this dialect is the tendency, on the part of the Friessisschers, to mute the d by opening the epiglottis. Whereas the Utrecht man will say *goot belemmerdt danket*, the Frieslander, as he is called in English, reveals a tendency to render the phrase thusly: *Goosesch blemmerdetsemt dett.*[33] This idiosyncrasy, according to modem philologists, derives from a physiological lack in the herrings which the Frieslander consumes in great quantities. The lack of proteins and of iodine – *particularly the lack of iodine* – sets up an etiological factor, heretofore unremarked, in the tissues of the windpipe, a phenomenon not unknown to those who are familiar with the habits of the sperm whale. When the whale comes up he blows. When the Frieslander speaks he is, *in lingua philologica*, but recapitulating the ontological defect of his mammal brother, the sperm whale. (See the addenda for further footnotes.)

Sunday, still aboard the Veendam.

Mannheim is the name of the crazy guy in the brig. As far as we know he is Dutch and, consequently, is being deported to his native land at the personal expense of the Queen. Mannheim is just crazy enough to know that he is entitled to special service. He has a special physician assigned to him and a wet nurse who wears a pink striped jacket. For the last three days Mannheim has been the center of attention. He stands at the porthole of his cell all day long, and sometimes far into the night, with a cigarette to his lips. When the cigarette burns down he rolls a bit of wet newspaper around it to make it last a little longer. He smokes only Pirate cigarettes which come from the Hague. When conversation lags Mannheim starts telegraphing with his signet ring. 'Operator, give me Asbury Park! This is Mannheim speaking. Hello! Is this O'Connell? I want the Philippine Islands.

Station WJK, No. 583.' He waits a few moments in order that the message may be relayed through the Malay Archipelago. After he gets the Philippines he says to me: 'What do you call those little statues from India... see nothing... hear nothing... and what's the last one? They are generally carved in ivory, what you call it. I once read a book about China. Yes, in the *Saturday Evening Post*. They are very strong... and *cruel*.'

The way to answer Mannheim is to talk about something else. About Greta Garbo for instance. *What do you think of Greta Garbo, Mannheim?* At this Mannheim throws his head back and gazes at the sky. A smile comes over his face – a cunning, malicious smile. 'Well,' he says, measuring his words, 'I tell you... it's like this... Greta Garbo is a great actress, a very great actress. She has what you call intelligence. She took all her money and put it Sweden – *before* the crisis! Chaplin is also a great artist. He does not need to talk... '

Just then a message comes – from the Antilles. Mannheim suspends all conversation, taps twice with the signet ring, and waits for an answer. 'Hello! O'Connell? This is Mannheim speaking. Place two destroyers up front! Clear all shipping through the Narrows. Throw the searchlights on. And put in, by the Queen's orders, an extra can of haarring... *Maatjes* haar-ring.' ... 'Now I tell you, about Greta Garbo... There is 24,000,000,000 dollars in gold down in the hold. Roosevelt knows nothing. He is the bellhop of Morgan and Rockefeller. I have made a big study of the whole question. I am an ethnolo-gist, what you call it. I make watches.'

Mannheim stops a moment and smiles – the oily, cunning, bland, elusive, hermaphroditic smile of the lunatic standing on the thresholds of lucidity. He knows that we are hanging on his words, that we expect something of him. His mouth is half open, he is about to say something. Suddenly he shuts his mouth firmly, the smile disappears. He was going to impart something to us, but he sees us grinning up at him and he decides that we are not worthy.

'So you are a psychologist,' says someone, just to get him started.

'Yes, I am a psychologist.'

'Where did you get your psychology... have you read Freud and Jung?'

'I got it from the same place they did – from the source.'

'They say you're crazy... is that true?'

'That's right. I am crazy. I am very crazy. I am vicious.'

'Would you like to get better?'

'No, I want to get worse... then I will be better. If you are sane then I want to be insane. Do you have a good job? Do you your meals regularly? You see, I am what you call...'

He interrupts himself. He looks up at the sky as though he were reading a private message. When he looks down again he has that cunning, malicious, ingratiating smile. It means that he is willing to humor us, to be crazy, if that's what we want him to be.

'Mannheim, I think you're plain nuts,' says Schwartz, who has a suspicion that Mannheim is only pretending to be crazy.

'I don't think you're capable of giving a straight answer to a straight question.'

'All right,' says Mannheim, 'ask me a few questions.'

'Who was Hamlet?' fires Schwartz.

'Hamlet... Hamlet... Let me see... Hamlet, that was Shakespeare. Let me see... *The Merchant of Venice*... No. That was Shylock... he wanted a pound of flesh.'

'Who did?'

'Macbeth.'

'Where are the Hottentots?'

'The Hottentots they come from Africa... near Zambezi.'

'Niagara Falls.'

'That's near Buffalo... for honeymooners.'

'Where is the obelisk?'

'The obelisk that is what you call hieroglyphics... Central Park.'

'How many languages do you speak?'

'Sixty-eight, without counting the dialects.'

'Have you got a stopwatch?'

'No, stop talking nonsense and you will have a stopwatch.'

At this point Mannheim seems to have had enough. He taps three times with his signet ring and then, in a loud, clear voice, he yells: 'MORNING DEVOTION!' And with that he throws out a pair of pajama drawers and a bath slipper.

'Mannheim, you're getting violent.'

'Yes, that is because I am crazy. I am vicious, you know.'

'How are you going to the dance tonight if you have no drawers.'

'I am going informal... Ask me some more questions... this is one of your clear moments.'

'How about women? Don't you get lonesome up there?'

'No, women are not my trouble. I have other troubles.'

'Like what?'

'To pass the time.'

'What happens to the hours we lose each day?'

'Eternity.'

'Good! A hundred percent!'

'Give me 98... that will be enough.'

The afternoon concert has commenced. There is an interruption. By now everybody is thoroughly relaxed. The violinist doesn't stand up anymore; he reclines on the bench with his feet sprawled on a chair, and plays without looking at the notes. The pianist is working like lightning. We are nearing Plymouth and there will be only one more concert before the passengers disembark. Just time enough to collect a tip from the outgoing passengers. The barriers are broken down, everybody is happy.

The ice broken at last, I feel like blowing the musicians to a drink. At the same time I feel that I am entitled to something special – if I blow them to a drink. I call the violinist over and ask him to play something genuinely Dutch. He shakes his head. 'We don't make any more music,' he says. A country without a music – that's impossible for me to imagine. All this *Katzenmusik*[34] they've been giving us comes from Germany, so he tells me. The Dutch have only folk music. I heard some of that last night: a Dutch carpenter was playing some Dutch Christmas carols. It was sad. Very sad. Even sadder than Anglo-Saxon Christmas music. There was also a society dame from the first class who did a tap dance for us. She had on high-heeled shoes. That was sad too. The only good thing about it was the tight skirt she wore – it showed off her beautiful ass.

I am writing this in the salon. Everybody is coming up to inquire if I have written something about them and what. The opera singer especially. She is half Spanish and half Dutch; her nationality is Russian. She would like me to write her biography when she stops singing, which will be in about three years now. She says last night the ceiling was too low and she was afraid of the high notes, that the ceiling would come down. There was a French singer too last night – a pain in the ass. She tried to sing like a milkmaid. Probably belongs to the Opera Comique. Anyway, she's just been asking me if I wouldn't mention something about the spring song she sang. It was called 'Primavera' – from the 16th century. The gist of it was, so she explains, not to bring the jug too often to the well.

I can see Mannheim from where I'm sitting. He looks troubled. He's just asked somebody how the barometer stands. He's all out of cigarettes too. The bar is closed down, until 3.30 – because it's Sunday. The musicians are standing near the bar waiting for it to open. They have promised to take only one drink apiece. Mannheim is rapping for me to come out and continue the conversation. He says I'm the most sympathic person on board. He says I'm intelligent too.

The violinist had just asked me if I had a good time on the trip and I said yes. So he says – WHEN? *Did you get that, Mannheim?*

I must go down now to make pipi. No use sitting down. Better blow it out with dynamite when we arrive at Boulogne. Now, the calmness of Scheveningen like an anaesthetic! The haarrings are rolling around in my gizzard, together with the *pommes rissolées* and the Nesselrode puddings. Tonight at seven the English will arrive with Alien Order Blanks which all passengers debunking at Plymouth are requested to fill out please. (Special notice to Mannheim: Do not fill out the Alien Order Blank. Go straight to Rotterdam by destroyer and report to the Queen's bellhop. O'Connell please stand by for further report!)

Somebody reports to me that Mannheim threatens to bring suit against me if I put him down in a book. Says he doesn't want to be photographed either...

Just had a short conversation with Mannheim. What were you doing in there? he says. Writing, I said. You can't do that, he says. You must consult me first. I've got to give you the title, otherwise it's no use. What are you going to say about me? You don't know what to put down yet – you haven't consulted me. Tonight I will introduce you to the doctor: he will tell you all about me. It will make you famous. But first I must see what you write. Then I will give you suggestions. We will corporate. I'll take 99% and split the rest with you fifty-fifty. You've got to work faster, because soon we will be in Plymouth. Wait a minute... I tell you what you must do... you must send it by cable. It's too late now to mail the story. Bring the pages to me and I'll cable them myself. I suppose you expect to make a lot of money, hein? If you're only writing for pleasure it's no use, it's a waste of time. Better tear it up. Besides, if you don't consult me you don't have any inspiration. Corporate with me and make a hundred cents on the dollar. Get me an apple now and some cigarettes – Pirate brand. I'm nervous today… the Queen is waiting for me… Put that down in your story.

At the table this evening I ask Herr Speck how much he intends to give the table steward by way of a tip. He says promptly: a dollar and a half. And how much to the room steward? A dollar and a quarter. He says the room steward was not so good – he forgot to put his name on the bath list twice. And what about the toilet room attendant? To him I will give 35 cents, says Herr Speck. He never did anything for me except to hand me a towel. I mention something about the brass rails. Humpf! grunts Herr Speck. I could make pipi even if they were not polished. De company should pay for dot!

The Zeelander at my left is going to visit his three brothers; they live in different parts of Holland. As they will have to take a day off when he goes to visit them he has decided to pay them each a day's wages according to the prevailing rate. Like that we will be quits, he says.

Everybody is excited now because land is in sight. Since it is only England I don't give a fuck. I've seen better land than this.

Mannheim has no precise plans. He only wants to get worse so that he will be sure of having his three meals a day and a place to sleep.

A sea gull has just dropped a little bird lime on a woman's jacket. It is the Lithuanian woman with the three noisy children. She says she will sue the company for a new jacket – *she knows her rights!*

Just had a short confab with Mannheim…

'What part of England are we passing?'

'The *southern* part!'

He laughs cunningly. And then adds: 'Tell me, are we not near the Isle of Wight?'

'I think so.'

'And the Isle of Man?'

'Yes.'

'Then where is the Isle of Women? Ha ha!'

I ask him if he won't give me his future address in Holland. 'Nothing doing!' he shouts.

'Then how will I be able to write you?'

'Don't bother!' he yells. 'It takes me only a minute and a half to make up my mind – forever. Send yourself a stamped envelope and put some elbow grease on it.' He smiles again, cunningly. 'Whatever you write,' he says, 'will be too late. I am the only one who can write the story for the newspapers. I have a patent on it.'

He throws me a cigarette box in which there is an orange peel. 'For the swallows!' he says. 'They are flying homeward with Madame Schumann-Heink. There is no duty on orange peels. Soon we will be getting rid of you crazy people. I will be the last man to go ashore. They will have a special carriage waiting for me at the pier. I am going to see the Queen... Aubergine she is called. She's a little daffy too, as you say. But her papers are in order. She usually travels first class, unless the weather is too hot.'

The minister from Kentucky is standing by the rail surrounded by his disciples. He is pointing out the land to them, as though they couldn't see it for themselves! He is describing the nature of the soil. Soon he will be talking again about the transepts, the naves, the apses. Some aisles are wide enough for thirty monks to pass abreast. Others are narrower. Above the lintel are the impediments where there is a clerestory. It's called a clerestory because you can see well from up there.

Now we are going to pass a big boat. Everybody out front to read what name is printed on it.

It was the Olive Bank, a windjammer with colored patches on the sails. Professor Went has just taken a snapshot of it. The professor has not yet spoken to a soul on board. I am wondering if he will stick it out to the bitter end. Probably will, being a professor. The opera singer has just arrived to tell me about the four-masted schooner. Too late, lady, I've got it down already! And now, as we are rapidly nearing Plymouth, where Mr Schwartz disembarks, I want to add for his information that if his brother should pirate my book please remember to put my name on the title page and not choose some half-assed idiot as illustrator. I don't want to go down to posterity, even in a pirated edition, as a 'pornographic' writer. Is that clear, Schwartz?

And a special memorandum to James Laughlin IV... Dear Laughlin: Please see that this letter is printed on handsome vellum... not more than fifty copies, numbered and signed by the author. Give half the royalties to Herr Manheim c/o Queen Aubergine, Scheveningen. Tell him to use the money for cigarettes – Pirate brand. If possible, put a silk cord through the binding, so that it looks like a dance program. Will append an addenda and an errata when I arrive at Boulogne.

And now, my dear Mannheim, a parting word to you... You can't imagine how sad I shall feel to leave you. You were the only person on board the boat for whom I felt a genuine sympathy. It's a pity that the others are not going to be locked up and you set free. The world would be much gayer and much freer if people like you were abroad. I wish I might have you beside me at the table tonight, in your pajama coat only, just as you stand when you cable to Honolulu, Singapore, Manila and points east. I would like you to come down just as you are, with the handcuffs around your 'pulses,' as you arrived the day before we sailed. I would like to split a haaring with you, a blue-and-white-striped one, if possible. Are your things all order? Have you brushed your teeth? So long, Mannheim, and God bless you! A pity we can't all go to the asylum. I'm sure we'd be much better off...

Addenda

On French soil at last! Home again! I must say a few words, before closing this letter, about the last lap of the voyage. I address this to all and sundry...

The moment we left Plymouth a great calm came over me. Plymouth itself is soothing to the nerves. England itself comes to a gentle resolution here at the land's end. She puts her best foot forward, and there's no boot and spur attached. It's green and gentle, dreamy, somnolescent. The earth seems to breathe, as at the very dawn of time. If only there were no English! They're hoving alongside now, the customs officials, the porters, and what not. They move slowly, smoothly, unostentatiously, with that irritating calm efficiency which always distinguished the English. I feel a hatred towards them instantly. Not hatred really, but a loathing. They seem like animated oysters. I feel the hard shell which conceals the flabby flesh: I feel their imperturbable possessivity. The oyster that tried to swallow the world! There is something ridiculous about them: they look subhuman. I look at the war vessels at anchor, the factories, the gas tanks, the lighthouse. They exist and therefore I assume the English made them – but it seems incredible. I can't think of the English as anything but ghouls and pirates – and such deucedly serious ones, you know. But the hell with them! I'm not getting off here...

Boulogne! The French! It comes with the tender – a clamor, a stridency, an anarchy, a nervous excitement entirely unjustified by the occasion. Nobody knows what's what, particularly the French. Even before one Frenchman steps aboard there is a confusion and a chaos such as only the most brilliant logic can produce. It's tonic and refreshing; at once the mind is exhilarated. It doesn't matter now *what* happens: something's happening, that's the important thing! We pull into the wharf amidst a tremendous flutter and jabber. You might almost imagine that they had been surprised by our arrival. Nothing works right. Nothing is in readiness. Or, so it seems. It's the French way, *and I love it*! They stand there looking at us as though it were a huge mistake, as though the tender had been sent out to fetch a load of cattle or green vegetables and behold! here comes a boatload of tourists laden with expensive luggage. What's to be done? Anyway they smell the tips coming. It seems to me I can see them smacking their lips. Perhaps I imagine it.

I'm standing at the rail, quietly enjoying the hubbub, the errors, the confusion, when suddenly I hear an officer shouting to a man on the quai, the man who directs the derrick which is to swing over our heads. I hear him shouting that the derrick should be adjusted so that it 'coincides,' etc... This word 'coincides' coming from the officer's lips gives me the most intense gratification. It has such a subtle, civilized ring. The language! At once I am in a mathematical world, a world where things are ordered Euclidically – and above all, *with justice*. Confusion and logic! A surface contradiction only. Fundamentally there is no contradiction. For that perfect equilibrium which the individual Frenchman represents there must be an external chaos matched by an internal order and precision all the more wonderful in that it is purely autonomous, that each one creates it for himself.

By the time the boat train reaches Creilly I am certain that we are in France. The coastal region gives one a dubious feeling; but the station at Creilly is beyond a doubt *French*. It is falling to pieces; it has never been repaired or painted since the day it was erected. It brings back to my memory the hotels I occupied during my long stay in France: the chairs that were held together by thongs, the tattered wallpaper, the patched carpet on the stairs, the broken windows, the armoires that could never be locked, the worn towels thin as tissue paper... Later, on my way to the Opera, this feeling comes over me again. A building is being torn down: I see the party wall, strips of blue-and-white wallpaper, flowers *en série*, the black mark of the chimney, the design of the stairway. A little farther off the name of a hotel strung along the façade in gilt letters a foot high, a name such as only the French could invent: *Hôtel d'Egypte et de Choiseul.* Choiseul – that means a street and a restaurant, and always evening; immediately after a cup of Brazilian coffee, drip by drip, with brass cups and a choice of pastry at the counter. Choiseul – it reminds me of Fustel de Coulanges, the little street near Val-de-Grâce. Choiseul – it reminds me never to ask Fred a question which demands a precise answer. It annoys him. So I never asked who or what Choiseul: it's a street and a restaurant towards evening, and immediately after a cup of Brazilian coffee, drip by drip...

Anyway, now at my elbow is a book which I picked up to glance at again: *Bubu de Montparnasse.*[35] The quaint French edition, with illustrations in the old manner. Holding this book in my hands is like embracing an old friend. I riffle the pages absent-mindedly: it seems as if the trees were shedding their leaves. I see the Seine, the quais, the narrow, winding streets with HOTEL prominently displayed, and of course, a man in a sack suit and bowler, the man slightly stooped, his mustache drooping. It is the year 1890 or so, a very important epoch astrologically, as Eduardo has just explained to me. I was born in this time of the grand conjunction – the Pluto–Neptune conjunction! My whole life is wrapped up in a little chestnut which fell off a tree during the years immediately preceding the dawn of a new century. I am at Louveciennes now. The lights have suddenly gone out. They are probably out in Paris too. The door won't close anymore, the hinges are rusty, the toilet seat is cracked and the paint rubbed off, the dining room walls are covered with mold.

Here the slightest inattention is costly, ruinous. Deterioration sets in quicker than in America. *Physical* deterioration. But the soul expands. Steadily, like a thermometer rising, the soul expands. Things are rotting away and in this quick rot the ego buries itself like a seed and blooms. No more the feeling of dry walls, of sharp divisions, of fracture and schism; here the body becomes the plant it is, it gives off its own moisture, creates its own ambiance, produces a flower. Every day now a new flower. The ego is rooted, the soil well manured. Instead of a million towering walls there is one great wall, the Chinese wall which the French have built out of their own blood. Within this wall a security and serenity unknown to America. Over there a fight each day to repair the dikes; each day one is fresh born, a babe which must mature by nightfall, and die.

America! How far away it seems now! Distance doesn't explain it. There's something else. When I think of New York I think I of a gigantic infant playing with high explosives. Not *new* so much *inhuman*. The whole of one's experience counts for naught. One awakes in the morning to look out on a virgin continent which has known no history. A clean jump, without transition, from barbarism to the dementia of Civilization. An external civilization, visible in knobs, bulbs, brackets, racks, screws, pulleys, steel, cement... How or why a skyscraper was erected thoroughly unimportant. It's there – that's all that matters! Facts! Facts! They hit you in the eye, they knock you cold, they trample on you. You walk amidst facts day in and day out. You sleep with the facts. You eat the facts. Supposing during a New York night all the marvels of Egypt, China, Carthage, Rome, Babylon were unrolled and left lying in the street. Supposing no one knew where they came from, how they got to what they signified. *That's New York!* It's the inside of a watch functioning perfectly in an incredible chaos. Not one man has been outside and had a look at the watch itself. Not one man knows what a watch is. The watch keeps perfect time. *What kind of time?* A question no American ever asks himself. It's time – or rather, it's a watch. Or a mechanism that would resemble a watch if there were something in the consciousness of the American which could imagine a watch. But there is none...

Looking now at *Bubu de Montparnasse* I recapture the image of the boulevard Sébastopol as it fixed itself in the back of my eye during the taxi ride. Leaving the Gare du Nord I had failed to notice the direction we were taking. I had hardly taken a glance at Paris. Suddenly I realized that we were on the boulevard Sébastopol. I looked deliberately at the shops, at the crowds, at individual men and women. Late afternoon and the sky is overcast. The whole street is registered in the back of my eye in sombre tones. It's not the overcast sky which causes it – it's something *in* the sky, something everlasting, a permanent effluvia given off by each individual citizen and by his ancestors in the grave. The boulevard Sébastopol is almost black. A soot black and not the gleaming Egyptian black which mirrors the lobbies of the skyscrapers. I look at the people on the sidewalk. They are black too. Black and decrepit. They are in tatters, like the dismantled wall lined with chimney stain and faded wallflowers. Only midafternoon and they are already black. They have been this way since morning. They will go to bed black. They will wake up black. The sky will stay overcast, it will rain again, and there will be bargain counters on the street and little black bags in which to carry the marketing. They will walk with one shoe on and one shoe off. A sou will count, will be counted carefully, even though it has a hole in it. Nothing will be thrown in the gutter – not even a banana peel. This man will ask for a light – in order to save a match. Tomorrow the situation will get worse. Yet not one man will dream of saying:

'*Away with it! Raze it clean!*' No one dares to dream of a new, fresh life, a life from scratch. No one dreams of a life without dirt, without poverty, without sorrow, misery, disease, death, disaster. All these elements are flowing through the street now in a black river, a sewer of despair that runs though the under- world where the ghosts and ancestors wander restlessly. So close are they, the men below, that the feet of those above are scraping the heads of those below. The graves are filled to overflowing, the dead are being disgorged. Somewhere at the edge there is a leak. Through this rift in the underworld there arises a gray vapor that turns the living world, living men, to soot black. The past breathes heavily down one's neck. It flutters and palpitates like a cape hiding a drowning man.

Between this and New York lies the ocean. The ocean is a clearance between the old and the new. When you take the boat you take a leap incalculable. If instead of a week the voyage lasted a month the boat itself, to say nothing of the passengers, would have disintegrated. We would arrive, either at Boulogne or New York, like a load of spoiled vegetables. No one would be able to gather himself together again. A death voyage without benefit of transfiguration.

Rolling along the boulevard Sébastopol in the late afternoon I feel somewhat spoiled. I am bringing my somewhat spoiled carcass to Paris. My soul I have not yet found...

It is only towards midnight, sitting in Roger's place, that I come to. We are sitting before the open window. The room is almost bare. I am looking out on the city of Paris – with two clear eyes. Just a windowful, *but it is Paris*. The boulevard Sébastopol must be there too. Perhaps one of those soft, jagged streets straggling through the thick foliage below is the boule- vard Sébastopol. Perhaps the same men and women are milling about. Perhaps they are in rags. Perhaps they have no shoes. Even if what I say were so it could not be true anymore. Not now! Now the lens is adjusted. Now I see straight. I see nothing anymore which is external – neither the walls, the clothes, nor the body itself. I see one big globule swimming in the blood of the great animal called MAN. This globule is Paris. I see it round and full, always the whole globule at once. If, closing the shutter, through the tiniest little fent I catch the back of a man, I see how and where it relates to the whole globule. Let him stand up straight, or let him bend over – it will always be a back, the back of a man. His back will never break through the globule. The globule will stretch and expand, permit the utmost freedom of movement, the most fantastic movements, *but it will not break*. The globule is always stronger than a man's back, stronger than the man himself, stronger than ten million men all pushing at once and in the same spot.

We are sitting in the little studio before the open window. The train is puffing along – the belt line which girdles Paris. No roar and whizz as it passes by. Just puffing along. Through an opaque ether it seems to move, through an elastic atmosphere which is the same up on the trestle as deep in the lungs. One atmosphere throughout: as difficult for the locomotive as it is difficult for the human lungs. The city is palpitating in the summer heat. The globule itself seems to be shrinking. The breath of the city is hot down our backs. Here I am in a room with old friends. I feel everything close, permeable, tangible, alive and breathing. I feel friendship itself, the essence of it slowly escaping through the stopped bottle, rising towards the envelope of the great globule which is shrinking. I feel the friendliness of the wine and of the carved cutlass which stands in a corner by the window. I say now what I have never said in America: *I feel a profound contentment.*

A moment ago, when I touched the book, I observed to myself that this profound contentment had not deserted me. Never before have I touched a book in this way. I feel that I am touching an old friend. A friend? Yes, suddenly it dawns on me – I am touching my old friend, the boulevard Sébastopol! How come then that I did not recognize my old friend immediately? Was the taxi outside the globule, trying vainly to pierce the envelope? Was it the envelope giving all the way, giving and giving until it seemed we were smothered in ethereal darkness? Where was I then? Now I am inside the globule. I realized it suddenly, sitting before the open window in Roger's studio. I entered by osmosis. I seeped through between late afternoon and midnight. *Inside* – I know it now. Sitting by the window, that first glance outdoors, perhaps it was then, that very moment, that I managed to get inside, to get inside all together, body and soul, the whole man.

I can't help thinking again of America. I remember now a night in New York when we were all drunk and suddenly someone burst out with this momentous phrase – '*But all great art is local!*' Nobody can possibly know, in America, what a phrase like this means. To be local there must be a sense of place, and there must be a whole to which the parts refer. America *seems* new because there is never a point of comparison. In reality there is no America! There are just millions of things unrelated one to the other, except as one part of a machine is related to another. To the parts themselves nothing seems new; an old watch which has stopped ticking can gaze in wonder at a new and moving part.

Yesterday I had to walk through the rue Bonaparte. I stopped off at a bistrot to inquire the whereabouts of a certain hotel. The same woman at the desk who greeted me years ago. She seems to recognize me. I seem to recognize her. Yes, I remember her well, remember when her belly was swollen, when she used to laugh so heartily that I thought she would burst a blood vessel. I remember too that she used to give the students credit – and still laugh heartily. I remember giving her too much money one day and I remember that she kept money for me until I came again. And now, though she seems recognize me, not a word out of her. Just that big smile which she had for every-body – and the hell with you if you croak tomorrow! I like it! It's French.

A little while ago, walking up the road, I pass a man standing in a field. He has a hoe in his hand and he is pottering around with it. He seems alone and complete, a sort of Chinese rock-bottom man. He is on one side of the fence and I am on the other. If I had dropped dead there in the road he would have gone on hoeing. He would hoe me into the sod, I believe. Well, anyway, I like it! I almost wish I had dropped dead… just to test it out.

And that brings me back to Mannheim, to the day when he started talking about China. I remember his opening words – 'Very cruel.' I thought of this often during the voyage. I thought of my countrymen who are so hospitable, so frank and gener-ous, so 'without rancor,' as Keyserling says. Yes, they are all that, but they are also cruel, a thousand times more cruel than the Chinese. They are the most inhuman torturers the world has ever seen. They are cruel in the way that children are cruel. They walk over you to reach for a new toy…

Passing the Lion de Belfort I catch the remains of a quarrel. A man is hanging on to a taxi and shouting at the chauffeur. He is white with rage. Behind his rage – and I see it just as clearly as if it were printed on a big banner – is the word JUSTICE. Never in America have I seen that kind of anger. I have seen violent quarrels, the most disgusting brutality, but never the white anger of outraged justice. The word is unknown and the feeling that accompanies it. Justice would tie up traffic. Justice would clog the machine. Ergo, away with it! I walk off without bothering to learn the cause of the quarrel. It's a classic quarrel here, and the cause is unimportant. But I saw the banner wave – *and that was important!*

With Justice goes philosophy, and that is what we had for dinner this evening. I felt this evening that I was talking again in a way that made sense. I was sitting in the mildewed dining room talking to Anaïs; Amelia, the half-wit, was running back and forth looking for *pimienta*. I suppose in New York I must have talked well too – now and then. But never like this. To speak well one must have an appreciative audience. One must be goaded to it. Anyway, we are sitting in the big globule, Anaïs and I, and we have only to put our hands out – everything of value is there within reach. Amelia is running back and forth: she is like an angel bringing me fresh subjects on a golden platter. Amelia is bringing in a whole rich platter of the past. It's right there in the kitchen, the past. No need for a telephone, or a radio. No need for a frigidaire. The past needs no ice. It needs only to be cured and hung in the wind. Do I want to re-examine my life? It's there in the kitchen and Amelia will bring it on a platter, along with the *pimienta*.

I have asked Amelia to bring in my old friend Doc Larsen. He was the one friend I had in America who had the possibilities of becoming a great human being. Amelia has brought him in, with the *pimienta*. We have him on the table now, a fresh roasted turkey, and Anaïs is putting a stopper over his mouth, the stopper which she bought in New York at the five-and-ten-cent store. As soon as the stopper is clapped over the bottle the bubbles rise from the bottom. We are putting the stopper over Doc Larsen. The words are rising in bubbles from the bottom. I know what he is gasping, but I can't hear. He is probably saying – 'a clean slate'... 'foundations for the revolution'... 'let the war come!' His words are imprisoned in the bottle. Doc, I want you to listen to me now! Somewhere there is a leak in you. Until it is repaired you can never become the great human being which you are. You have swallowed the whole world and, if you could hold it for just a little while, for a half hour, say, you would be great, immense, *colossal*. But that leak – you must find where it is! You are dribbling away. Every day you slaughter a million words. Yes, Doc, you're a slaughterhouse of words. An abattoir! Everything you say about the world is correct. You are correct in everything. But until that leak is repaired you won't change even a pin. You lie in bed listening to your heart. You say your heart is bad, you say you may croak any day. I say you're a liar. Your bad heart is just an excuse. You are exploiting your bad heart in the name of revolution. Before the automobile accident you were on the way. You ran your legs off ministering to the sick. Your presence alone was sufficient to heal your patients. People felt your sympathy, your tremendous vitality, your loving curiosity. Now you say sympathy is no good – you want to spread intelligence. That's where you make a terrible mistake. I know you would like to object here, but I'm not going to let you. I've got the stopper on and I mean to keep it on. Look, in the other room there is a book case. Thousands of books in there – and not one of them could cure you. Curious, I was thinking of that a little while ago, standing in front of a book whose title arrested me. *Un Malade lmmortel* it was called. I thought of you, of the revolution, of the whole American people now in the throes of a blight such as never before visited the human race. Doc, forget about the spread of human intelligence! The world is intelligent enough – *too intelligent*, as a matter of fact. A little more sympathy, that's what's needed. Better to be wrong, better to be unjust, than to turn your back on sympathy. A moment ago, as I said, I was prowling back and forth, glancing at the titles of the books. Old friends they are to me, and most of them I have never opened. Most of them I will never open, I feel sure. But I picked up one book, didn't I? I picked up *Bubu*. And I read a few paragraphs here and there – enough to last me for the rest of my life. I am sure if you had *Bubu* in your hand you would give up riding in taxis and walk the streets the whole day long. Here, I want to show you an illustration from the book. You see that little boat passing under the bridge? That's a *bateau mouche*,[36] and the bridge is the *Pont au Change*. On this very page it is written – '*Sommes-nous à Paris? Nous sommes en haut des airs, dans un pays d'eau, mais dont l'air gronde comme des voitures qui roulent.*'[37] It is twilight and Maurice and Big Jules are passing a bistrot. Big Jules is leaning over Maurice, who is *Bubu de Montparnasse*. And where is Montparnasse? No matter about that... *Bubu* is still alive, and the year 1890 something with him. Nobody can tear this off the calendar. It is a Sabbatical year!

All this I'm telling you because during the dinner we were discussing the role of the physician. Like everything else that belonged to the *human* world the physician too is rapidly disappearing. The tall buildings again! No flock to tend, no fold to look after. He has no orbit and hence no ties. No responsibilities and no sympathy. He doesn't bother to cure anymore – he is only interested in exploiting his private theories. He is interested in the theory of medicine, not in the art of therapy. The great physician was the little family doctor who didn't know his ass from his elbow, but he always came with a little satchel and some pills, and when he laid his hand on your pulse you felt better immediately. The family doctor worked miracles. The modern quack can't even cure his own child. Nobody has faith in him, nor has he any in himself. He raises people from the dead and they spit on him afterwards. He dies of overwork in the prime of life. His whole life is spent in a vacuum, so that when he dies there is nothing left to clean up. I couldn't advance a single proof of all this, except that it is so – *a fact!*

The point? Oh yes, *sympathy*. Walking down the rue Bonaparte the other day, illogical as it may seem, I caught on to it again. When you walk down this street you know it's all shit what the intellectuals are saying – that art is dead, that there is no audience, etc. This little street is the proof of what I say. Anything said away from this street is a lie. This street lets you live. The day you walk down this street you'll know what I'm talking about all the time. That day the leak in your side, or wherever it is, will be stopped. *I guarantee it*. If not, you had better shoot yourself! That's my last word to you and to America. *Schöne Grüsse!*[38]

Well, Fred, how was that? I'm going to stop now and let you praise the shit out of me. Tell them what a genius I am – from America sent.

Via Dieppe–Newhaven

The thing was that I wanted to be among English-speaking people again, for a little while at least. I had nothing against the French; on the contrary, I had at last made a bit of a home for myself in Clichy and everything would have been swell if it hadn't been for the fact that I had just gone through a crisis with my wife. She was living in Montparnasse and I was living with my friend Fred, who had taken an apartment, in Clichy just outside the Porte. We had agreed to separate; she was going back to America as soon as the money arrived for the boat fare.

So far so good. I had said goodbye to her and I thought everything was finished. Then one day when I walked into the grocer's the old woman informed me that my wife had just been in with a young man and that they had taken away a good supply of groceries which they had charged up to my account. The old woman seemed a bit perplexed and a little worried too. I told her it was OK. And it was OK too, because I knew my wife didn't have any money, and after all a wife has to eat just like any other person. About the young man, that was OK too: he was just a fairy who felt sorry for her and I supposed he had put her up for the time being in his apartment. In fact, everything was OK except that she was still in Paris, and when in Christ's name was she going to beat it, that's what I was wondering about.

A few more days passed and then she dropped in one late afternoon to have dinner with us. Why not? We could always scrape up a bit of food whereas in Montparnasse among the riff-raff she was obliged to hang out where food was almost unobtainable. After the dinner she got hysterical: she said she was suffering from dysentery ever since she had left me and that it was my fault, that I had tried to poison her. I walked her to the Metro station at the Porte without saying a word. I was sore as hell, so goddamned sore that I couldn't talk. She was sore too, sore because I refused to argue the matter with her.

I thought to myself, walking back, well this is the last straw, she surely won't come back again. I poisoned her. Good, if she wants to think that way let her! That ought to settle the issue.

A few days later I had a letter from her asking for a little cash with which to meet the rent. Seems she wasn't living with the fairy at all, but in a cheap hotel back of the Gare Montparnasse. I couldn't give her the money immediately as I didn't have any myself so I let a few days intervene before going to her hotel and settling the bill. While I was trotting round to her hotel a pneumatique had come for me saying that she simply must have the money or she'd be kicked out. If I had had a little money I wouldn't have put her to all these humiliations, but the point is I didn't have any. However, she didn't believe me. And even if it were true, she said, I could at least have borrowed it for her. Which was also true. But I was never good on borrowing large sums; all my life I had been used to asking for hand-outs, for chicken feed, and feeling damned grateful when I got that. She seemed to have forgotten that. It was natural enough that she should because she was bitter and her pride had been wounded. And to do her justice I must add that had the situation been reversed the money would have been forthcoming; she always knew how to raise money for me but never for herself. That I've got to admit.

I was getting pretty wrought up about the whole thing. I felt like a louse. And the worse I felt the less I was able to do. I even suggested that she come back and stay with us until the money which she was expecting for the boat trip should come. But this she wouldn't hear of, naturally. Or was it natural? I was so damned perplexed and humiliated and confused that I didn't know any more what was natural and what wasn't. Money. Money. All my life it had been a question of money. I would never be able to solve the problem and I didn't hope to.

After turning round and round like a rat in a trap I got the brilliant idea of beating it myself. Just walk out on the problem, that's always the easiest way. I don't know how the idea came to me but suddenly I had decided that I would go to London. If you had offered me a château in Touraine I would have said no. For some reason or other I had made up my mind that it must be London and no other place. The reason I gave myself was that she'd never think of looking for me in London. She knew I hated the place. But the real reason, as I soon discovered, was that I wanted to be among English-speaking people; I wanted to hear English spoken twenty-four hours of the day, and nothing but English. In my weak condition that was like falling back on the bosom of the Lord. Talking and listening to English meant just that less strain. God knows, when you're in a jam to talk a foreign language, or even just to listen to it – because you can't shut your ears even if you try to – is a subtle form of torture. I had absolutely nothing against the French, nor against the language they spoke. Up until she arrived on the scene I had been living in a sort of Paradise. Suddenly everything had gone sour. I found myself muttering things against the French, and against the language particularly, which I would never have dreamed of thinking in my sober senses. I knew it was my own fault, but that only made it worse. Well, London then. A little vacation and perhaps by the time I returned she would have left. That's all there was to it.

I rustled up the dough for a visa and a return trip ticket. I bought a visa for a year thinking that if by any chance I should change my mind about the English I might go back a second or a third time to England. It was getting on towards Christmas and I began to think what a jolly old place London might be during the holidays. Perhaps I would find a different sort of London than the one I knew, a Dickensian London such as tourists always dream of. I had the visa and the ticket in my pocket and just about enough dough to last me for ten days. I was feeling almost jubilant about the trip.

When I got back to Clichy it was almost dinner time. I walked into the kitchen and there was my wife helping Fred with the dinner. They were laughing and joking as I walked in. I knew that Fred wouldn't say anything to her about my going to London and so I sat down to the table and laughed and joked a bit myself. It was a jolly meal, I must say, and every-thing would have gone off splendidly if Fred hadn't been obliged to go to the newspaper office after dinner. I had been canned a few weeks ago but he was still working, though expecting the same fate any day. The reason I was canned was that, even though I was an American, I had no right to be working on an American newspaper as a proofreader. According to French theory the job could just as well have been held by a Frenchman who knew English. That griped me a bit and no doubt contributed to my feeling sour towards the French the last few weeks. Anyway, that was over and done with and I was a free man again and I would soon be in London talking English all day long and far into the night if I wanted to. Besides, my book was coming out very soon and that might change everything. All in all things weren't half as black as they had seemed a few days back. Thinking how nicely I was going to duck the whole thing I got a bit careless and ran out, in a moment of exuberation, to buy a bottle of Chartreuse which I knew she liked better than anything. That was a fatal mistake, The Chartreuse made her mellow and then hysterical and then reproving. We sat there at the table, the two of us, and I guess we rehearsed a lot of things that should have been forgotten. Finally I got to such a point of guilt and tenderness that I blurted out the whole thing – about the trip to London, the money I had borrowed, and so on and so forth, I forked the whole thing out and laid it on the table. There it was, I don't know how many pounds and shillings, all in bright new English money. I told her I was sorry and to hell with the trip and tomorrow I would try to get a refund on the tickets and give that to her too.

And here again I must render her justice. She really didn't want to take the money. It made her wince, I could see that, but finally she accepted it reluctantly and stuffed it away in her bag. As she was leaving she forgot the bag and I was obliged to run down the stairs after her and hand it to her. As she took the bag she said goodbye again and this time I felt that it was the last goodbye. She said goodbye and she stood there on the stairs looking up at me with a strange sorrowful smile. If I had made the least gesture I know she would have thrown the money out of the window and rushed back into my arms and stayed with me for ever. I took a long look at her, walked slowly back to the door, and closed it. I went back to the kitchen table, sat there a few minutes looking at the empty glasses, and then I broke down and sobbed like a child.

It was about three in the morning when Fred came back from work. He saw right away that something had gone wrong. I told him what had happened and then we sat down and ate, and after we had eaten we drank some good Algerian wine and then some Chartreuse and after that a little cognac. It was a damned shame, in Fred's opinion, and I was a fool to have forked up all the money. I agreed, but I felt good about it just the same.

'And what about London? Do you mean to tell me you're not going to London?' he says.

'No,' I said, 'I've given up the idea. Besides, I couldn't go now even if I wanted to. Where's the dough to come from?'

Fred didn't seem to think the lack of dough was any grave obstacle. He thought he could borrow a couple of hundred francs at the office and on pay-day, which was only a few days off, he would wire me more. We sat there discussing the thing until dawn, and of course drinking a bit too. When I hit the hay I could hear the Westminster chimes – and a few rusty sleigh bells too. I saw a beautiful blanket of snow lying over dirty London and everybody greeting me with a hearty 'Merry Christmas!' – *in English*, to be sure.

I made the Channel crossing at night. It was a miserable night and we stayed indoors shivering with the cold. I had a hundred franc note and some change – that was all. The idea was that as soon as I found a hotel I was to cable and Fred would cable back some more dough. I sat at the long table in the salon listening to the conversation going on around me. The thought uppermost in my mind was how to make the hundred francs stretch as far as possible, because the more I thought about it the less sure I was that Fred would raise the dough immediately. The scraps of conversation I picked up also had to do with money. Money. Money. The same thing everywhere and all the time. It seems that England had just that day paid her debt to America, much against her will. She had kept her word, as they were saying all about me. England always kept her word. And more of that and more, until I felt like strangling them for their bloody honesty.

I hadn't intended to break the hundred franc note until absolutely necessary, but with this silly conversation going on about England keeping her word and knowing that they had spotted me as an American I finally got so jumpy that I ordered a beer and a ham sandwich. That brought me directly into contact with the steward. He wanted to know what I thought about the situation. I could see that he thought it was a bloody crime what we had done to England. I felt sore that he should make me responsible for the situation just because I happened to be born an American. So I told him I didn't know anything about the situation, that it was none of my affair, and further- more that it was a matter of absolute indifference to me whether

England paid her debts or didn't pay her debts. He didn't relish this very much. A man ought to have an interest in the affairs of his country, even if his country is in the wrong, that's what he thought. I told him I didn't give a damn about America or Americans. I told him I didn't have an ounce of patriotism in me. At that moment a man who had been pacing up and down beside the table stopped to listen to me. I had a feeling that he was a spy or a detective. I piped down almost at once and turned to the young man beside me who had also called for a beer and a sandwich.

Apparently he had been listening to me with some interest. He wanted to know where I came from and what I was going to do in England. I told him I was taking a little vacation, and then, impulsively, I asked him if he could recommend a very cheap hotel. He said he had been away from England quite a long while and that he didn't know London very well anyhow. Said he had been living in Australia the last few years. Just then the steward happened along and the young man interrupted himself to ask the steward if he knew of any good cheap little hotel in London. The steward called the waiter over and asked him the same question, and just as he put the question to the waiter the man who looked like a spy came along and paused a moment to listen in. From the serious way in which the subject was discussed I could see at once that I had made a mistake. One shouldn't ask questions like that of a steward or a waiter. I felt that they were looking me over suspiciously, that they were giving my pocket-book the X-ray. I tossed off the beer at one gulp and, as though to prove that money was the least of my worries I called for another and then, turning to the young man at my elbow, I asked him if he wouldn't let me buy him a drink too. When the steward came back with the drinks we were deep in the wilds of Australia. He started to say something about a hotel but I told him immediately to forget about it. It was just an idle question, I added. That seemed to stump him. He stood there a few moments not knowing what to do, then suddenly, moved by some friendly impulse, he blurted out that he would be glad to put me up in his own home at Newhaven if I cared to spend the night there. I thanked him warmly and told him not to worry about it any more, that I would go on to London just the same. It really isn't important, I added. And the moment I said it I knew that that too was a mistake, because somehow, despite myself, I had made the thing seem quite important to everybody.

There was still a bit of time to kill and so I listened to the young Englishman who had had a strange time of it in Australia. He was telling me of his life as a sheep herder, how they castrated I don't know how many thousands of sheep in a day. One had to work fast. So fast, in fact, that the most expedient thing to do was to grab the testicles with your teeth and then a quick slit with the knife and spit them out. He was trying to estimate how many thousand pair of testicles he had bitten off in his hand to mouth operation during his sojourn in Australia. And as he was going through his mental calculations he wiped his mouth with the back of his hand.

'You must have had a strange taste in your mouth,' I said, instinctively wiping my own mouth.

'It wasn't as bad as you might imagine,' he answered calmly. 'You get used to everything – in time. No, it wasn't a bad taste at all… the idea is worse than the actual thing. Just the same, I never thought when I left my comfortable home in England that I would be spitting out those things for a living. A man can get used to doing most anything when he's really up against it.'

I was thinking the same thing. I was thinking of the time I burned brush in an orange grove in Chula Vista. Ten hours a day in the broiling sun running from one fire to another and the flies biting like mad. And for what? To prove to myself that I was a man, I suppose, that I could take it on the chin. And another time working as gravedigger: to show that I wasn't afraid of tackling anything. The gravedigger! With a volume of Nietzsche under his arm, and trying to memorize the last part of Faust to and from work. Well, as the steward says, '*the English never twist you!*' The boat is coming to a stop. Another swig of beer to drown the taste of sheep's nuts and a handsome little tip for the waiter just to prove that Americans pay their debts too sometimes. In the excitement I find myself quite alone, standing behind a bulky Englishman with a chequered cap and a big ulster. Landing in any other country the chequered cap would look ridiculous, but as it's his own country he can do as he pleases, and what's more I almost admire him for it, it makes him seem so big and independent. I'm beginning to think that they're not such a bad race after all.

On deck it's dark and drizzly. The last time I pulled into England, that was coming up the Thames, it was also dark and drizzly and the faces were ashen grey and the uniforms were black and the houses were grim and grimy. And up High Holborn Street every morning I remember there passed me the most respectable, lamentable, dilapidated paupers God ever made. Grey, watery paupers with bowlers and cutaways and that absurd air of respectability which only the English can muster in adversity. And now the language is coming to me a little stronger and I must say I don't like it at all: it sounds oily, slimy, servile, unctuous. I feel the class line cutting through the accents. The man with the chequered cap and the ulster has suddenly become a pompous ass; he seems to be talking Choctaw to the porters. I hear Sir all the time. Can I do this, *Sir*? Which way, *Sir*? Yes, *Sir*, No, *Sir*. Bugger me if it doesn't make me a bit creepy, all this yes sir and no sir. *Sir my ass*, I say under my breath.

At the Immigration Office. Waiting my turn on the line. The rich bastards go first, as usual. We move up inch by inch. Those who passed through are having their baggage inspected on the quay. The porters are bustling about loaded down like donkeys. Only two people ahead of me now. I have my passport in my hand and my train ticket and my baggage checks. Now I'm standing square in front of him, offering him my passport. He looks at the big white sheet beside him, finds my name and checks it off.

'How long do you intend to stay in England, Mr Miller?' he says, holding the passport in his hand as though ready to give it back to me

'A week or two,' I answer.

'You're going to London, are you?'

'Yes.'

'What hotel are you stopping at, Mr Miller?'

I have to smile at this. 'Why, I don't know,' I respond, still smiling. 'Perhaps you can recommend me a hotel.'

'Have you any friends in London, Mr Miller?'

'No.'

'Just what are you going to do in London, if I may ask?'

'Why, I'm going to take a little vacation.' Still smiling.

'I suppose you have enough money for your stay in England?'

'I think so,' says I, still nonchalant, still smiling. And thinking myself what a cinch it is to bluff it through with questions like that.

'Do you mind showing me your money, Mr Miller?'

'Of course not,' and reaching into my jeans I haul out the remains of the hundred franc note. The people next to me are laughing. I try to laugh too, but I'm not very successful. As for my inquisitor, he gives a feeble little chuckle and looking me square in the eye he says with all the sarcasm he can put into it: 'You didn't expect to stay very long in London on that, did you, Mr Miller?'

Always this *Mr Miller* tacked on to every phrase! I'm beginning to dislike the son-of-a-bitch. What's more it's beginning to get uncomfortable.

'Look here,' I say, still amiable and still outwardly noncha-lant, 'I don't intend to have a vacation on that. As soon as I get a hotel I expect to wire for money. I left Paris in a great hurry and... '

He cuts me short. Can I give him the name of my bank in Paris, he wants to know.

'I haven't got a bank account,' I'm obliged to answer. That makes a very bad impression I realize at once. I can feel the hos-tility growing up all about me. People who were holding their bags are putting them down now, as though they knew they were in for a long siege. The passport which he had been holding in his hands like a little testament he puts on the counter before him and holds it there, like a damaging piece of evidence, with outstretched fingertips.

'Where were you going to get the money from, Mr Miller?' he ask more blandly than ever.

'Why, from a friend of mine, the man who lives with me in Paris.'

'Has he a bank account?'

'No, but he's got a job. He works on the *Chicago Tribune*.'

'And you think he will send you the money for your vacation?'

'I don't think so, I know so,' I answered tartly. 'I'm not trying to give you a cock and bull story. I told you I left in a hurry. I left with the understanding that he'd send me the money as soon as I arrived in London. Besides, it's my money, not his.'

'You left your money with him rather than put it in a bank, is that it, Mr Miller?'

'Well,' I said, beginning to lose my temper, 'it isn't a hell of a lot of money and besides, I don't see the point of all this. If you don't believe me I'll stay right here and you can send a cable and find out for yourself.'

'Just a minute, Mr Miller. You say the two of you live together... do you live in a hotel or in an apartment?'

'An apartment.'

'And the apartment is in your name?'

'No, in his. That is, it belongs to the both of us, but it's in his name because he's a Frenchman and it makes it easier.'

'And he keeps your money for you?'

'No, not usually. You see, I left under rather unusual circumstances. I... '

'Just a minute, Mr Miller,' and he motions to me to step back from the ranks a bit. At the same time he calls one of his assistants over and hands him my passport. The latter takes the passport and goes behind a screen some distance off. I stand there watching the others go through.

'You might go and have your baggage inspected meanwhile,' I hear him say as if in a trance. I move off to the shed and open my luggage. The train is waiting for us. It looks like a team of Eskimo dogs straining at the leash. The locomotive is puffing and steaming. Finally I walk back and take my stand in front of my interlocutor. The last few passengers are being hustled through the examination.

Now the tall thin man from behind the screen comes forward with the passport in his hand. He seems determined in advance that I'm a malefactor.

'You're an American citizen, Mr Miller?'

'Obviously,' I answer. With this guy I know there's going to be no mercy. He hasn't a speck of humour in him.

'How long have you been in France?'

'Two or three years, I guess. You can see the date there for yourself... *Why?* What's that got to do with it?'

'You were thinking of spending several months in England, were you?'

'No, I wasn't. I was thinking of spending a week or ten days there, that's all. But now... '

'So you bought a visa for a year, thinking to spend a week.'

'I bought a return trip ticket too, if that interests you.'

'One could always throw the return ticket away,' he says with a malicious twist of the mouth.

'One could if he were an idiot. I don't get the point. And anyway, look here, I'm tired of all this nonsense. I'm going to stay in Newhaven overnight and take the next boat back. I don't have to spend my vacation in England.'

'Not so fast, Mr Miller. I think we ought to look into this a little more closely.'

As he said this I heard the whistle blow. The passengers were aboard and the train was just starting. I thought of my trunk which had checked through to London. Nearly all my manuscripts were in it, and my typewriter too. A nice mess, I thought to myself. All because of that chicken feed I slapped down on the counter.

The little fat fellow with the bland imperturbable mask now joined us. He seemed to be expecting a treat.

Hearing the train roll out of the station I resigned myself to inquisition. Thinks I to myself, now that they've fucked me, let's see how far they can prolong the agony. First of all, however, I demanded my passport back. If they wanted to grill me a little more OK. There was nothing to do at that hour of the night and before turning in at Newhaven I thought I'd go through with the song and dance.

To my amazement the tall thin fellow refused to return my passport. That made me furious. I demanded to know if there was an American Consul on hand. 'Listen,' I said, 'you may think what you like, but that passport belongs to me and I want it back.'

'There's no need to get excited, Mr Miller. You'll have your passport before you leave. But first there are a few questions I'd like to put to you… I see that you are a married man. Is your wife living with you – and your friend? Or is she in America?'

'I don't see that that's any of your business,' I said. 'But since you brought the subject up I'm going to tell you something now. The reason I came away with so little money is because I gave the money for my trip to my wife before leaving. We're separating and she's going back to America in a few days. I gave her the money because she was broke.'

'How much money did you give her, if I may ask?'

'You're asking so damned many questions that you have no right to ask I don't see why you shouldn't ask that too. If you want to know, I gave her about sixty pounds. Let's see. I may still have the exchange slip in my wallet... ' And I made a gesture as if to reach for my wallet and look for the slip.

'Wasn't that rather foolish to give your wife all that money and come to England penniless, or almost so?'

I gave him a sour smile. 'My dear man, I've tried to explain to you that I'm not coming to England as a pauper. If you had let me go to London and wire for the money everything would have been all right. I suppose it's a waste of time to say a thing like this to you but try to understand me, will you? *I'm a writer*. I do things impulsively. I don't have bank accounts and I don't plan things years in advance. When I want to do something I do it. For some reason or other you seem to think that I want to come to England to... frankly, I don't know what the hell's in your mind. I just wanted to come to England to hear English, if you can believe it – and partly too to escape my wife. Does that make sense to you?'

'I should say it does,' says the tall thin fellow. 'You want to run away from your wife and let her become a public charge. How do you know she won't follow you to England? And how will you take care of her in England – without money?'

I felt as though I were talking to a stone wall. What was the use of rehearsing the whole thing again? 'Listen,' I said, 'as far as I'm concerned I don't care what happens to her. If she becomes a public charge that's her affair, not mine.'

'You're working for the *Chicago Tribune*, you say?'

'I never said anything of the kind. I said my friend, the man who was to send me the money, *he's* working on the *Chicago Tribune*.'

'You never worked for the newspaper then?'

'Yes, I used to work for them, but I don't now. They fired me a few weeks ago.'

He snapped me up immediately. 'Oh, then you *did* work for the newspaper in Paris?'

'Didn't I just say so? Why? Why do you ask?'

'Mr Miller, could I see your carte d'identité... I suppose you *have* a carte d'identité, living in Paris, as you say.'

I fished it out for him. The two of them looked it over together.

'You have a non-worker's card – yet you worked for the *Chicago Tribune* as a proofreader. How do you explain that, Mr Miller?'

'No, I suppose I can't explain that to you. I suppose it's useless to explain to you that I'm an American citizen and that the *Chicago Tribune* is an American newspaper and that therefore... '

'Excuse me, but why were you dismissed from the newspaper?'

'That's just what I was coming to. You see, the French officials, those who have to do with the red tape, seem to take the same attitude as you do. Perhaps I could have remained on the *Tribune* if I hadn't also been a bad proofreader. That's the real reason why I was fired, if you want to know.'

'You seem rather proud of the fact.'

'I am. I think it's a mark of intelligence.'

'And so, not having a job on the *Tribune* any more you thought you'd come to England for a little vacation. And you provided yourself with a visa for a year and a return trip ticket.'

'Also to hear English and to escape my wife,' I added.

Here the little round-faced fellow spoke up. The tall fellow seemed ready to relinquish the tussle.

'You're a writer, Mr Miller?'

'Yes.'

'You mean you write books and stories?'

'Yes.'

'Do you write for the magazines in America?'

'Yes.'

'Which ones… can you name a few?'

'Certainly. The *American Mercury*, *Harper's*, *Atlantic Monthly*, *Scribner's*, *the Virginia Quarterly*, *the Yale Review*… '

'Just a minute.' He walked back to the counter and bending down he pulled out a big fat directory. '*American Mercury*… *American Mercury*… ' he kept mumbling as he thumbed the pages. 'Henry V. Miller, isn't it? Henry V. Miller… Henry V. Miller… Was it this year or last year, Mr Miller?'

'It may be three years ago – for the *Mercury*,' I said blandly.

Apparently he had no book on hand that went back that far. Couldn't I give him the name of a magazine I had written for in the last year or two? I said no, I had been too busy writing a book the last or so.

Had the book been published? What was the name of the American publisher?

I said it had been published by an Englishman.

What was the name of the publisher?

'The Obelisk Press.'

He scratched his head. 'An *English* publisher?' He couldn't seem to remember any English house by that name. He called his sidekick who had disappeared behind the screen with my passport. 'Ever hear of the Obelisk Press?' he yelled.

At this point I thought it timely to tell him that my English publisher published from Paris. That seemed to make him hopping mad. An English publisher in Paris! It was a violation of the rules of nature. Well, anyway, what were the names of the books?

'There's only one,' I said. 'It's called *Tropic of Cancer*.'

At this I thought he would throw a fit. I didn't know what had come over him for the moment. Finally he seemed to bring himself under partial control and, in the suavest, the most sarcastic voice imaginable, he said: 'Come, Mr Miller, you don't mean to tell me that you write medical books too?'

It was my turn to be flabbergasted. The two of them were standing there boring me through with their mean gimlet-like eyes.

'*The Tropic of Cancer*,' I said slowly and solemnly, 'is *not* a medical book.'

'Well, what is it then?' they asked simultaneously.

'The title,' I answered, 'is a symbolic title. The Tropic of Cancer is a name given in textbooks to a temperate zone lying above the Equator. Below the Equator you have the Tropic of Capricorn, which is the south temperate zone. The book, of course, has nothing to do with climatic conditions either, unless it be a sort of mental climate. Cancer is a name which has always intrigued me: you'll find it in zodiacal lore too. Etymologically it comes from chancre, meaning crab. In Chinese symbolism it is a sign of great importance. The crab is the only living creature which can walk backwards and forwards and sideways with equal facility. Of course my book doesn't treat of all this explicitly. It's a novel, or rather an autobiographical document. If my trunk were here I might have shown you a copy. I think you'd be interested in it. By the way, the reason it was published in Paris is because it's too obscene for England or America. Too much cancer in it, if you know what I mean... '

This brought the discussion to a close. The tall slim fellow packed his brief case, put on his hat and coat and waited impatiently for the little fellow to get ready. I asked for my passport again. The tall slim fellow went behind the screen and got it for me. I opened it and I saw that he had drawn a big black X through my visa. That infuriated me. It was like a black mark against my good name. 'Where's a place to put up for the night in this burg?' I asked, putting as much snot and venom in it as I could muster.

'The constable here will take care of that,' says the big fellow, giving me a wry smile and turning on his heel. And with that I see a very tall man dressed in black with a big helmet and a cadaverous face coming towards me out of the gloom of the far corner.

'What do you mean?' I yelled. 'Do you mean that I'm under arrest?'

'No, I wouldn't say *that*, Mr Miller. The constable will put you up for the night and in the morning he'll put you on the boat for Dieppe.' And he started to walk away again.

'OK,' I said. 'But you're going to see me back here, maybe next week.'

By this time the constable was at my side and had me by the arm. I was white with rage, but that firm grasp of the arm told me it was useless to say anything more. It was like the hand of death itself.

As we walked towards the door I explained very calmly to the constable that my trunk had gone on to London and that it contained all my manuscripts as well as other things.

'We can take care of that, Mr Miller,' he says in a quiet, low, steady voice. 'Just step this way with me,' and he made for the telegraph office. I gave him the necessary dope and he assured me in his quiet, easy voice that I'd have my things in the morning, the first thing in the morning. I knew from the way he spoke that he was a man of his word. Somehow I had an instant respect for him. I did wish, however, that he'd let go my arm.

Shit, I wasn't a criminal, and even if I did want to make a break for it where would I go? I couldn't jump in the sea, could I? However, it was no use starting things with him. He was a man who obeyed orders and it was enough just to take one look at him to know that he had been trained like a dog. He escorted me gently and firmly to the hoosegow. We had to pass through a number of vacant, dimlit rooms or halls to get to the joint. Each time we opened a door he paused and, taking out a bunch of keys, locked the door behind us. It was impressive. I began to get a bit of a thrill out of it. It was ridiculous and awesome at the same time. Christ knows what he would have done if I had been a really dangerous criminal. I suppose he'd have manacled me first. Anyway, finally we got to the hoosegow, which was a sort of big gloomy waiting room very dimly lit. There wasn't a soul in the place, nothing but a few long empty benches, as far as I could make out.

'Here's where we spend the night,' said the constable in the same quiet, steady voice. Really a gentle voice it was. I was beginning to take a liking to him. 'There's a washroom in there,' he added, pointing to a door just in back of me.

'I don't need to wash up,' I said. 'What I'd really like to do is to take a crap.'

'You'll find the place in there,' he answered, and opening the door he turned on the light for me.

I went in, took my coat off and sat down. Suddenly, as I was sitting there I looked up and to my amazement there was the constable sitting by the doorway on a little stool. I wouldn't say he was watching me, but certainly he had one eye on me, as they say. At once my bowels were paralyzed. *That*, I thought to myself, that beats everything! And then and there I made a mental note to write about the incident.

As I was buttoning up I expressed a little of my amazement. He took what I said in good part, replying very simply that it was part of his duty. 'I've got to keep you under observation until I hand you over to the captain in the morning,' he said. 'Those are the orders.'

'Do people try to run away sometimes?' I asked.

'Not very often,' he said. 'But things are very bad now, you know, and lots of people are trying to get into England who don't belong here. People who are looking for work, you know.'

'Yes, I know,' I said. 'Things are in a mess.'

I was pacing slowly up and down in the big waiting room. Suddenly I felt rather chilly. I went over to the big bench where my overcoat was lying and flung it around my shoulders.

'Would you like me to build you a fire, sir?' the constable suddenly asked.

I thought it was damned considerate of him to ask a question like that and so I said, 'Why, I don't know. How about you? Do you want a fire too?'

'It isn't that, sir,' he said. 'You see the law entitles you to a fire, if you wish it.'

'The hell with that!' I said. 'The question is, would it be a bother to make one? Perhaps I can help you.'

'No, it's my duty to make you a fire if you wish it. I have nothing to do but look after you.'

'Well, if that's the case, let's have a fire,' I said. I sat down on the bench and watched him getting it started. Pretty decent, I thought to myself. So the law entitles you to a fire. Well, I'll be goddamned!

When the fire was made the constable suggested that I stretch out on the bench and make myself comfortable. He dug up a cushion from somewhere and a blanket. I lay there looking at the fire and thinking what a strange world it is after all. I mean how on the one hand they manhandle you and on the other hand they nurse you like a baby. All written down in the same book, like debit and credit columns in a ledger. The government is the invisible bookkeeper who makes the entries, and the constable is just a sort of human blotter who dries the ink. If you happen to get a kick in the ass or a couple of teeth pushed down your throat that's gratis and no record is made of it.

The constable was sitting on the little stool by the fireside reading the evening paper. He said he would just sit there and read a bit until I fell asleep. He said it in a neighbourly way, without the slightest malice or sarcasm. A different species entirely from the other two bastards whom I had just left.

I watched him reading the paper for a while and then I started to talk to him, in a human way, what I mean, not like he was the constable and me the prisoner. He was not an unintelligent man, nor did he lack sensibility. He struck me, in fact, very much like a fine greyhound, something anyway with blood and breeding. Where those other two farts, who were also doing their duty by the government, impressed me as a couple of sadistic jakes, as mean, low, cringing bastards who enjoyed doing their dirty work for the government. I'm sure if the constable were to kill a man in the line of duty you could forgive him for it. But those other pimps! Bah! I spat into the fire with disgust.

I was curious to know if the constable ever did any serious reading. To my surprise he told me that he had read Shaw and Belloc and Chesterton – and some of Somerset Maugham's work. *Of Human Bondage* was a great book, he thought. I thought so too and I scored another strike for the constable on my mental blackboard.

'And you're a writer too?' he said, very gently, almost timidly, thought.

'A bit of a one,' I said diffidently. And then impulsively, falteringly, stutteringly, I launched into an account of *Tropic of Cancer*. I told him about the streets and the cafes. I told him how I had tried to put it all in the book and whether I had succeeded or not I did know. 'But it's a *human* book,' I said, getting up from the bench and moving very close to him. 'And I tell you one thing, constable, you impress me as being very human too. I've enjoyed this evening with you and I want you to know that I have a respect and admiration for you. And if you don't think it's immodest of me why I'd like to send you a copy of my book when I get back to Paris.'

He wrote his name and address in my notebook and told me he would read the book with great pleasure. 'You're a very interesting man,' he said, 'and I'm sorry we had to meet under such painful circumstances.'

'Well, let's not talk about that,' I said. 'What do you say we do a wink of sleep now? Eh?'

'Why yes,' he said, 'you can make yourself comfortable on the bench there. I'll just sit here and doze a bit. By the way,' he added, 'would you like me to order breakfast for you in the morning?'

I thought to myself well that's a pretty swell guy, about as decent as they make 'em. And with that I closed my eyes and dozed off.

In the morning the constable took me aboard the boat and handed me over to the captain. There were no passengers aboard yet. I waved goodbye to the constable and then I stood at the prow of the boat and took a good look at England. It was one of those quiet, peaceful mornings with a clear sky overhead and the gulls flying. Always, looking at England from the sea, I am impressed by the gentle, peaceful, somnolent quality of the landscape. England comes so gently down to the sea, it's almost touching. Everything seems so still, so civilized. I stood there looking at Newhaven with tears in my eyes. I wondered where the steward lived and whether he was up and eating his breakfast or pottering around the garden. In England every man *ought* to own a garden: it's meant to be that way, you feel it immediately. As I say, it couldn't have been a better day and

England couldn't have looked lovelier, more inviting, than she looked at this moment. I thought of the constable again and how he fitted into the landscape. I want him to know, if he ever reads this, how much I regret the fact, seeing how gentle and sensitive he was, that I had to take a crap in front of him. If I had ever dreamed that he was going to sit there and keep an eye on me I would have held it in until we got to sea. I want him to know that. As for the other two bastards, I want to warn them here and now that if ever I encounter them again in this life I am going to spit in their eye. And may the curse of Job be on them for the rest of their lives. May they die in agony in a foreign land!

One of the most beautiful mornings I have ever known. The little village of Newhaven nestling in the white chalk cliffs. The end of the land, where civilization slips quietly into the sea. I stood there in a reverie for a long while, and a profound peace came over me. In such moments it seems that everything that happens to you happens for the best. Standing there quiet and peaceful like that I got to thinking of our own New Haven (Connecticut), where I had gone once to visit a man in gaol. He was a man who had worked for me as a messenger and we had become friends. And then one day in a fit of jealousy he had shot his wife and then himself. Fortunately both of them recovered. After they had transferred him from the hospital to the prison I went to see him one day; we had a long talk through a steel mesh. When I left the prison I suddenly remarked how beautiful it was outdoors and, acting on the impulse, I went to a beach nearby and took a dip. I was one of the strangest days I ever spent at the ocean. When I dove off the springboard I had a feeling that I was taking leave of the earth for ever. I didn't try to drown myself, but I didn't care a hoot if I were to drown. It felt marvellous to dive off the earth, to leave behind me all that man-made muck which we glorify with the word civilization.

Anyway, as I came up and swam around I seemed to be looking at the world with new eyes. Nothing was like it had been before. People looked curiously separate and detached; they were sitting around like seals drying themselves in the sun. What I'm trying to say is that they seemed absolutely devoid of significance. They were just part of the landscape, like the rocks and the trees and the cows in the meadows. How they had ever assumed such a colossal importance on this earth was a mystery to me. I saw them plainly and distinctly as natural objects, as animals or plants. I felt that day that I could commit the most dastardly crime with a clear conscience. A crime without reason. Yes, it was that that I felt strongly: to kill some innocent person without reason.

As soon as the boat turned its nose towards Dieppe my thought began to take a different turn. I had never been out of France before and here I was returning in disgrace with that black mark against my visa. What would the French think? Perhaps they would begin to cross-examine me too. What was I doing in France? How did I make my living? Was I taking bread out of the mouths of French workers? Was I apt to become a public charge?

Suddenly I got into a panic. Supposing they refused to let me return to Paris? Supposing they transferred me to another boat and shipped me back to America? I got into a terrible funk. America! To be shipped back to New York and dumped there like a load of rotten apples! No, if they were going to try that stunt I'd jump overboard. I couldn't bear the thought of returning to America. It was Paris I wanted to see again. Never again would I grumble over my lot. It wouldn't matter if I had to live the rest of my life in Paris as a beggar. Better a beggar in Paris than a millionaire in New York!

I rehearsed a marvellous speech, in French, which I intended to make to the officials. It was such an elaborate, melodramatic speech that the crossing of the Channel passed like a dream. I was trying to conjugate a verb in the subjunctive when suddenly I saw the land popping up and the passengers flocking to the rail. Now it's coming, I thought. Brace up, me bucko, and unloose the subjunctives!

I stood apart from the others instinctively, as though not to contaminate them. I didn't know just what the procedure would be in stepping off – whether there'd be an *agent* to meet me or whether somebody would just pounce on me with the grappling hooks as I hit the gangplank. It was all much more simple than my anxiety led me to anticipate. As the boat pulled into the wharf the captain came forward, and grasping me by the arm just as the constable had done, he led me to the rail where I was in plain view of the men ashore. When he had caught the eye of the man on the quay whom he was seeking he raised his left hand aloft with the index finger pointing heavenward and then motioned to me. It was like saying *One!* One head of cabbage today! One head of cattle! I was more amazed than ashamed. It was so direct and logical, too, that you could hardly quarrel about it. After all, I was on a boat and the boat was pulling in and I was the man they were looking for and why send a cablegram or telephone when all you need to do is raise your arm and point like that? What could be simpler, less expensive?

When I observed the man whom I was being delivered to my heart sank. He was a big brute of a fellow with black handlebars for moustache and an enormous derby which half crushed his big appetizing ears. Even at long range his hands looked like big hams. And he too was dressed all in black. Clearly things were against me.

Walking down the gangplank I was struggling desperately to recall fragments of the speech which I had rehearsed only a few moments ago. I couldn't remember a blooming phrase. All I kept saying to myself was – 'Oui, monsieur, je suis un

Américain – mais je ne suis pas un mendiant. Je vous jure, monsieur, je ne suis pas un mendiant.'[39]

'Votre passeport, s'il vous plait!'

'Oui, monsieur!'

I knew I was destined to say 'Oui, monsieur' over and over again. Each time it came out of me I cursed myself for saying it. But what are you going to do? That's the first thing that's drummed into you when you come to France. *Oui, monsieur! Non, monsieur!* You feel like a cockroach at first. And then you get used to it and you say it unconsciously, and if the other fellow doesn't say it you notice it and you hold it against him. And when you're in trouble that's the first thing that pops out of your mouth. '*Oui, monsieur!*' You say it like an old billy-goat.

Anyway, I had only said it once or twice, because like the constable this chap was also a silent man. His duty consisted, as I happily discovered, in nothing more than escorting me to the office of another official who again demanded my passport and my carte d'identité. Here I was politely asked to sit down. I did so with a great feeling of relief and at the same time, taking a last look at the big brute who had dismissed me, I asked myself – where have I seen that man before?

After the grilling of the night before one great difference made itself felt immediately: *Respect for one's individuality!* I think now that even if he had put me on a boat for America I would have accepted my fate tranquilly. There was an inner order to the language, for one thing. He said nothing capricious, nothing insolent, nothing mean or foul or vindictive. He was talking the language of his people and there was form in it, an inner form which had come out of a deep experience of life. It was all the more striking, this clarity, in comparison with the external chaos in which he moved. In fact, it was almost ridiculous, this disorder which enveloped him. It was not altogether ridiculous because what inspired it was human, human foibles, human fallibilities. It was a disorder in which you feel at home, which is a purely French disorder. He had, after a few entirely perfunctory questions, left me undisturbed. I still had no idea what my fate was to be, but I knew definitely that whatever his verdict it would not be capricious or malevolent. I sat there in silence observing the way he went about his work. Nothing seemed to work just right, neither the pen, nor the blotter, nor the ink, nor the ruler. It was as though he had just opened the office and I was his first client. But he had had other offices before, thousands of them, and so he was not greatly perturbed if things didn't go smoothly all at once. The important thing, as he had learned, was to get it all down correctly in the proper books. And to have the necessary stamps and seals which were to give the case its legal, orthodox aspect. *Who was I? What had I done? Ça ne me regard pas!*[40] I could almost hear him saying it to himself. All he had asked me was – where were you born? Where do you live in Paris? When did you come to France? With those three facts in his hand he was constructing a beautiful little dossier in my name to which he would finally sign his name with the proper flourish and then affix the stamps with the proper seal. That was his job and he understood thoroughly.

It took him quite a little while to go about this task, I must admit. But time now was all in my favour. I would have sat there until the next morning quietly watching him if it had been necessary. I felt that he was working in my interest and in the interest of the French people and that our interests were one because clearly we were both intelligent and reasonable and why would either of us want to cause any one any trouble? I suppose he was a man whom the French would call a *quelconque*, which is not quite the same as a nobody in English, because Mr Anybody or Everybody in France is quite another species from Mr Nobody in America or England. A *quelconque* is not a nobody in France. He is a man like any other man, but he has a history and a tradition and a race behind him which often makes him more than the so-called Somebodies in other countries. Like this patient little man working on my dossier these men are often shabbily dressed: they look ragged about the edges and sometimes, be it said, they are not very clean either. But they know how to mind their own business, which is a very great deal.

As I say, it took him a little while to transcribe this data from one record to another. There were carbons to be adjusted, receipts to be detached, little labels to be pasted on, and so forth. Meanwhile the pencil had to be sharpened, a new stub had to be inserted in the penholder, the scissors had to be found, and they were found finally in the waste basket, the ink had to be changed, a new blotter dug up... there were lots of things to be done. And to complicate matters he discovered at the last minute that my French visa had expired. Perhaps it was out of delicacy that he merely suggested that it would be a good thing if I were to renew my visa – in case I intended to travel out of France again, he said. I was only too delighted to fall in line with the suggestion, feeling at the same time, however, that it would be a long time before I would ever think of leaving France again. I gave my consent more out of politeness and consideration for his valiant efforts on my behalf.

When everything had been put in order and my passport and carte d'identité were safely in my pocket again I very respectfully suggested that we have a little drink together at the bar across the way. He very graciously accepted the invitation and together we sauntered leisurely out to the bistrot opposite the station. He asked me if I liked living in Paris. A little more exciting than this hole, eh? he added. We didn't have time for much of a conversation as the train was due to leave in a few minutes. I thought perhaps at the end he would say – 'How did you ever come to get into such a mess?' – but no, not the slightest allusion to the subject.

We walked back to the quay and as the whistle blew we shook hands cordially and he wished me a bon voyage. As I took my seat he was still standing there. He waved his hand and again he said: 'Au revoir, Monsieur Miller, et bon voyage!' This time the *Monsieur Miller* sounded good to my ears, and perfectly natural. In fact it sounded so good and natural that it brought tears to my eyes. Yes, as the train rolled out of the station I distinctly remembered, two big tears roll down my cheeks and falling on to my hands. I felt safe again among human beings. The 'bon voyage' was ringing in my ears. *Bon voyage! Bon voyage!*

A light drizzle was falling over Picardy. It made the thatched roofs look invitingly black and the grass a little greener. Now and then a patch of ocean veered into sight, to be swallowed up immediately by rolling sand dunes, then farms and meadows and brooks. A silent, peaceful countryside where each man minds his own business.

Suddenly I felt so goddamned happy I wanted to stand up and shout or sing. But all I could think of was '*bon voyage!*' What a phrase that! All our lives we're knocking about here and there mumbling that phrase which the French have given us, but do we ever take the *bon voyage*? Do we realize that even when we walk to the bistrot, or to the corner grocer, that it's a voyage from which we may never return? If we keenly felt that, that each time we sailed out of the house we were embarking on a voyage, would it make our lives a little different? While we make the little trip to the corner, or to Dieppe, or to Newhaven, or wherever it may be, the earth too is making her little trip, where nobody knows, not even the astronomers. But all of us, whether we move from here to the corner or from here to China, are making a voyage with our mother the earth, and the earth is moving with the sun and with the sun the other planets too are moving... Mars, Mercury, Venus, Neptune, Jupiter, Saturn, Uranus. The whole firmament is moving and with it, if you listen closely, you will hear 'Bon Voyage!' 'Bon Voyage!' And if you get still as a needle and don't ask a lot of foolish questions you will realize that to make a voyage is only an idea, that there is nothing in life but voyage, voyage within voyage, and that death is not the last voyage but the beginning of a new voyage and nobody knows why or whither, but *bon voyage* just the same! I wanted to stand up and sing that in the key of Ut-Mineur. I saw the whole universe like a network of tracks, some deep and invisible like the planetary grooves, and in this vast misty slithering to and fro, in the ghost-like passage from one realm to another, I saw all things animate and inanimate waving to another, the cockroaches to the cockroaches, the stars to the stars, man to man, and God to God. All aboard for the big trek to nowhere, but *Bon Voyage* just the same! From osmosis to cataclysm, all a vast, silent and perpetual movement. To stand still within the big crazy movement, to move with the earth *however* she wobbles, to join up with the cockroaches and the stars and the gods and men, that's voyaging! And out there in space where we are moving, where we leave our invisible tracks, out there is it possible that to hear a faint, sarcastic echo, a slimy, anaemic little English voice asking incredulously – 'Come, Mr Miller, you don't mean to say that you write *medical* books too?' Yes, by Jesus, now I can say it with a clean conscience. Yes, Mr Nobody from Newhaven, I do write medical books too, marvellous medical books which cure all the ills of time and space. In fact, I am writing now, this very minute, the one great purgative of the human consciousness: *the sense of voyage!*

And just as I imagined I saw the idiot from Newhaven cocking his ear to hear me better a big shadow loomed in front of him and blotted him out. Just as I was about to say to myself – 'Where have I seen this face before?' – it dawned on me like a flash. The man with the moustache at Dieppe, that face I had seen somewhere before, I recognized it now: it was the face of Mack Swain! He was The Big Bad Wolf and Charlie was Samson Agonistes. That's all. I just wanted to straighten it out in my mind. *Et bon voyage. Bon voyage à tout le monde!*

Notes

Aller Retour New York

1. Alfred Perlès (1897–1990), writer, most famous for his associations with Henry Miller, Lawrence Durrell and Anaïs Nin in the Parisian literary scene of the 1930s. Miller and Perlès rented a flat together in Clichy in 1933, and remained lifelong friends, each writing to and about the other, most notably in Perlès' *My Friend Henry Miller* (1955) and Miller's *Joey* (1979).

2. Miller and Perlès called one another Joey. In *My Friend Henry Miller* Perlès writes, 'Henry thought it simplified matters and, moreover, taught one to be humble.'

3. Ignacy Paderewski (1860–1941), Polish pianist and composer. He was elected president of Poland's provisional parliament in 1940.

4. Gypsy Rose Lee, born Louise Rose Hovick (1914–70), stripper, actress and writer.

5. June Mansfield Miller (1902–79) became Henry Miller's second wife.

6. Ernest Hemingway (1899–1961), novelist and short-story writer; Joseph Schrank (1900–84), writer for both stage and screen. Miller was a frequent visitor to Joe and his wife Bertha's apartment in Paris in 1931.

7. The logo of the National Rifle Association incorporates an eagle.

8. *The Ego and Its Own* (*Der Einzige und sein Eigentum*, 1844), German philosopher Max Stirner's main work.

9. Blaise Cendrars, pseudonym of Frédéric Louis Sauser (1887–1961), writer, poet and traveller, who wrote in a fluid, impressionistic style. He was a part of the artistic scene in Montparnasse, and was friends with Hemingway and Miller.

10. The St Johns River is Florida's longest river, and one of the longest rivers in the United States that flows in a northward direction. Juan Ponce de Léon (*c.*1460–1521) was a Spanish conquistador, and in 1513 the first European to 'discover' Florida.

11. Me neither, because with those people, why not. They take me for a dirty Jew too (French).

12. Sir James Jeans (1877–1946), British astrophysicist; Sir Arthur Eddington (1882–1944), British astronomer. Both men were renowned popularisers of science.

13. Oswald Spengler (1880–1936), philsopher of history and author of *The Decline of the West*.

14. Potato dumpling (although Miller has mistakenly used the plural form here) (German).

15. Small, sweet (French).

16. *Journey to the End of the Night* (1932, trans. 1934), first and best-known novel by Louis-Ferdinand Céline (1894–1961).

17. Henri Barbusse (1873–1935), French novelist.

18. *Of Time and the River* (1935), by American novelist Thomas Wolfe.

19. Claude Farrère (1876–1957), prolific French novelist.

20. Ezra Pound (1885–1972), American poet and critic; Gertrude Stein (1874–1946), American writer, central to the Parisian avante-garde scene; Miguel de Unamuno (1864–1936), Spanish philosopher and writer.

21. 1932 prose work by the American poet and novelist William Carlos Williams (1883–1963).

22. 1914 volume of poetry by Gertrude Stein (see note 19).

23. Hermann Graf Keyserling (1880–1946), Baltic German philosopher. His widely read book *America Set Free* was published in the United States in 1929.

24. 'Immer Oder Nimmer' means literally 'Always or never'. 'Oder Nimmer Oder Schwimmer' is nonsensical; Miller is probably simply playing with words (German).

25. Triple metre (German).

26. 'Do you speak French, madame, or sir?' (French).

27. This is probably Miller's phonetic spelling of *was goed* or rather *het was goed*, meaning 'it was good' (Dutch).

28. One is kindly requested not to throw anything into the toilets that could block them up or hinder the flow of water (Dutch).

29. 'I have never made anybody happy… including myself… that's how I was born.' (Dutch)

30. Keno is a game similar to bingo. The Dutch here should read *achten-tachtigen* and *zesenzestigen*, which translate as 'eighty-eighting' and 'sixty-sixing': the sum of the cards needed to win.

31. 'Vest with stripey trousers in (or 'and') a modern design' (amalgamation of French/Dutch/German).

32. This line and its 'translation' are Miller's fabrication, as is, presumably, the name of the poet.

33. Both of these phrases appear to be Miller's creations, but are probably variants of 'thank you'.

34. Literally 'cat music' (German).

35. 1901 novel by French writer Charles-Louis Philippe.

36. The local nickname for sightseeing boats on the Seine (French).

37. 'Are we in Paris? We're high up in the air, in a country of water, but where the air roars like cars on the move.' (French).

38. Kind regards! (German).

Via Dieppe–Newhaven

39. 'Yes, sir, I'm an American – but I'm not a beggar. Honestly, sir, I am not a beggar.' (French).

40. It doesn't concern me! (French).

Biographical note

Henry Valentine Miller was born in 1891 in New York, the son of a tailor, and brought up in Brooklyn. He was a good pupil at school, but left the City College of New York after only two months' attendance, after which he took various odd jobs and travelled in south-western America and Alaska, supporting himself with the money that was meant to put him through Cornell University.

Miller's first book, *Clipped Wings*, was published in 1922; in 1924 he left his job, married his second wife, June Smith, and devoted himself to a life of writing. He left America for Europe in 1930 and settled in Paris, where he met Anaïs Nin, Lawrence Durrell and Alfred Perlès, with whom he lived in Clichy, and various other members of the Parisian literary scene. His auto-biographical novel *Tropic of Cancer*, a candid account of life as an artist in Paris, was published in France in 1934, but was banned for many years in both the United States and Britain, on grounds of obscenity. Further significant works include *Black Spring*, *Tropic of Capricorn*, *The Colossus of Maroussi* and the series of three novels *Sexus*, *Plexus* and *Nexus*, together known as *The Rosy Crucifixion*.

On the outbreak of the Second World War Miller returned to the United States, eventually settling in Big Sur, California. He continued to write until his death in 1980.